SPSS: THE BASICS

Kamal Heidari (Ph.D)

Hamid Reza Hashemi (Ph.D)

ISBN: 1514320436
ISBN-13: 978-1514320433

TO
OUR DEAR PARENTS FOR THEIR SUPPORT AND LOVE

CONTENTS

FOREWORD

SPSS, standing for *Statistical Package for the Social Sciences*, is a powerful, user-friendly software package for the manipulation and statistical analysis of data. The package is particularly useful for students and researchers in psychology, sociology, psychiatry, and other behavioral sciences, containing of both univariate and multivariate procedures much used in these disciplines. However, it is often heard that the students cannot handle and work efficiently with this package and the books compiled or translated about this software could not delineate the basic parts of SPSS and the way they operate. The present volume is a solution to this problem.

Who is this book for?

In general terms, this book is for anyone new to SPSS. No prior knowledge of statistics or mathematics is needed, or even expected. In specific terms, this book was written with two groups in mind: students who are not majoring in mathematics but are instructed to use SPSS, and office workers who are instructed to use SPSS to analyze some data. For most people who generate statistics, the complexity of using the software becomes an obstacle. Our purpose in writing this book was to show you how to move that obstacle out of the way with minimum effort.

How the book is organized

This book was written so you could read first; the basic parts of the package, to get yourself started with SPSS, and second; jump around to the main parts and programs as needed. SPSS is miscellaneous software, and we don't claim to illuminate everything. However, we do claim that those programs and aspects which are often employed by students have been explained in detail. The book features step-by-step procedures that you can follow to see how SPSS operates. After you use the provided sample data and step through an example, you'll have a handle on how to apply those steps to your data. The parts of the book divide the information about SPSS into its major categories. The chapters in each part further divide the information into smaller subcategories.

CHAPTER ONE

An Overview of Research Concept

When the early human beings came into this world, they had very little or no knowledge as to the world around them. They needed to know more and more about the world into which they had stepped. That is, they tried to research more and more about everything in detail. To achieve this, scads of ways and methods were used in order to enhance their knowledge and as a result, have a better quality of life. As time elapsed, more developed and effective procedures were employed by different people. All these ways and methods, from the simplest one to the most sophisticated one, are considered as research methods.

From the above-cited statements it can be inferred that the concept of research is not something new. But since the creation of human beings, research, in various forms, has been used by them. Therefore, knowing about this integral part of life is, in fact, a necessity. As it was already noted, the main purpose of doing researches is to increase the amount of knowledge. But what do we actually mean by the word "knowledge"? To put it simply, knowledge is a collection of facts or theories about different things and phenomena which enable us to understand something or solve a problem. To clarify this definition, a simple example can be a great help. We know that one effective way to cure the cold disease is to drink different warm soups. Knowing that drinking warm soups is beneficial in treatment of cold is, in fact, a piece of knowledge. Knowledge is obtained through doing researches. Therefore, now it is time to see what research is.

Definition of Research

Among various mentioned definitions for the concept of research, the one brought up by Farhady (1994) simply conveys all that needs to be said. He defines research as a systematic approach to find answers for questions. There are three key words in the definition: systematic approach, answers, and questions. First, research is a systematic approach. By systematic approach it means that in order to do a research some specific and fixed steps need to be taken. That is, we can not do a reliable research without careful consideration of what our purpose of doing the research is, how we want to collect the data from which the final conclusions and as a result, the new piece of knowledge are obtained. The second and third key words are question and answer. There should be a question, so that we follow a systematic approach to find answer for it.

Educational Research

Educational research is one kind of research designed to solve problems that arise in the domain of education and to add to human new body of knowledge in this area. Based on Pallant (2005), educational research is divided into two main categories: quantitative research and qualitative research. Quantitative research refers to those researches which are based on numeric data and aim at studying the relationship among variables. In contrast, qualitative research is one that is based on non-numeric data and aims at understanding different social phenomena. The main differences of quantitative and qualitative researches have been summarized in Table 1-1.

Table 1.1 quantitative and qualitative research differences

	Quantitative research	Qualitative research
Purpose	To study relationship among variables	To understand social phenomena
Design	Developed prior to study	Evolving during study
Approach	Deductive, test theory	Inductive, generate theory
Tools	Using standard instruments	Using face-to-face interactions
Sample	Large samples	Small samples
Analysis	Numeric statistical analysis	Narrative descriptions and interpretations

esearch question

It was already mentioned that one of the most important aspects of a research is to have a question to which we want to find an answer. This question is referred to as research question. In other words, research question is one of the most important aspects of a research, especially a quantitative research that determines the purpose of the research. According to Ary, Jacobs, and Razavieh (2002), a good research question should have the following characteristics:

- It must be researchable

- It must be suitable for the researcher
- It must be ethical
- It must lead to new problems and questions
- Its answer must contribute to the body of knowledge in education

Hypothesis

Hypothesis is actually the tentative answer to the research question. In other words, the researcher's probable answer to the research question or his prediction about the probable outcomes of the study is called hypothesis. There are two main types of hypotheses. The first type is called null hypothesis which refers to the hypothesis that assumes neither a positive no a negative relationship among variables. In our researches, we usually try to reject a null hypothesis. A simple example for null hypothesis may be *"using on-line feedback or traditional feedback makes no difference in the improvement of students' writing skill"*. The second type of hypothesis is alternative hypothesis which poses either a positive or negative relationship among variables. An example for alternative hypothesis is *"using on-line feedback is more effective than traditional type of feedback in improving the students' writing skill"*. Depending on whether a positive or a negative relationship is assumed, alternative hypothesis is further divided into two subcategories of positive and negative hypotheses respectively.

Variable

In any research, particularly in quantitative research, the researcher considers two or more variables and tries to study the relationship among them. Variable simply means anything that varies. In educational research, it refers to any feature and attribute that varies from one person to another, or from an object to another. Being left handed or right handed is an example of variable. In education research, examples of variable may be motivation, intelligence, anxiety, etc. There are different types of variable in terms of their function. The main types of variables are independent variable, dependent variable, moderator variable, controlled variable, and intervening variable.

Independent variable is the one that affects another variable. Dependent variable is one type of variable which is affected by independent variable. If we want to examine the effect of on-line feedback on students' writing skill, then on-line feedback is the independent variable and students' writing skill is considered as the dependent variable. Moderator variable is one kind of independent variable that is used to modify the relationship between independent and dependent variables. If in the above-cited example, we suppose that on-line feedback is more effective for males than females, gender is then a moderator variable. Control variable is the factor(s) we want to control in order to neutralalize its effect in the study. If in a study, the researcher uses just left-handed people as his subjects, it is a control variable. Finally, intervening or extraneous variable refers to a factor which may affect the outcomes of the study but is out of our control.

Scales of measurement

It was already noted that in quantitative researches, we deal with measurable variables which are usually referred to as scales or levels of measurement. As Brown (1988) says, scales are actually names for the different ways of observing, organizing, and assigning numbers to data, which makes them important for understanding the entire data collection process. The four main types of these scales of measurement are briefly explained below:

Nominal scale

As its name indicates, nominal (or categorical) scales are used for naming and categorizing data. One important point about nominal scale is that the numbers used in it are just values and labels. That is, they have no mathematical value and are used just to identify different members from each other. A simple example for nominal scale is the players of a soccer team. Each member has a number. These numbers are used just to discriminate the players from each other and have no mathematical value. The point needs to be mentioned here is that if the nominal scale has just two levels, it is called a dichotomous scale. A case in point for dichotomous scale is gender which includes just two levels (male or female).

Ordinal scale

Ordinal scales or rank-ordered scales are used not only for categorizing data, but for the ranking and ordering them. A simple example of ordinal scale is ranking the students from the best to the worst in terms of their scores. In an ordinal scale, then, each point on the scale is ranked as "more than" and "less than" the other points on the scale. The points are then lined up and numbered as first, second, third, and so on.

Interval scale

A variable measured on an interval or continuous scale contains not only the same information as an ordinal scale does, but interval scales have an equal distance between subsequent values. Temperature degrees are good examples for this kind of variable. There is equal distance between 90° and 100° as there is between 42° and 32°. Another example is students' scores. The difference between 16 and 17 is equal to that of 19 and 20. Another basic feature of interval scale is that it has an arbitrary zero point. That is, if a person gets zero on a test, it doesn't mean that he/she know nothing.

Ratio scale

Ration scale is another kind of scale of measurement which is mostly used in physical sciences. The main reason is that it has an absolute zero. The example is weight. When we say that an object weighs zero; it means that it has no weight at all.

Likert scale

This kind of scale is frequently used in research reports in TESL/TEFL and social sciences in general. It is usually used in questionnaires where a special kind of survey question uses a set of ordered responses. An example of Likert scale is as follow:

Impoliteness is more important than politeness

1. Strongly agree   2. Agree   3. Neutral   4. Disagree   5. Strongly disagree

Population, sample, parameters, and statistics

Based on Ary, Jacobs, and Razavieh (2002), population refers to all members of a well-defined group of people, events, or objects. For example, if we want to study the effect of on-line feedback on Iranian EFL learners, the population is all the Iranian EFL learners all over the country. However, since it is actually impossible to include all members of a population in the study, a sample of the population is used. Sample, then, refers to a limited fraction of population which represents the main features of population. Each feature of population and sample is called parameter and statistic respectively.

Effect size

The framework for testing whether the intended effects in a study are genuine or not has some problems. The first problems is about how significant is the effect. In other words, just knowing that a test statistic is significant doesn't mean that the effect is meaningful. To resolve such a problem, it is a good idea to measure the size of the effect we are testing, that is, its **effect size**. In general, an **effect size** is the magnitude of the impact of the independent variable on the dependent variable. Effect size gives researchers the information that they may have thought they were getting from a null hypothesis significance test, which is whether the difference between groups is important or negligible. An effect size, in other words, is simply an objective and standardized measure of the magnitude of the observed effect. Effect sizes are useful because they provide an objective measure of the importance of the effects. By saying that the measure is standardized it means that it is possible to make a comparison among effect sizes across studies that have measured different variables or have used different scales of measurement. A range of measures of effect size has been proposed;

the most common of which is the one suggested by Cohen (1988). Cohen suggested the following criteria for concluding if an effect is small, medium, or large.

$r = .10$ (**small effect**), in this case the effect explains 1% of the total variance

$r = .30$ (**medium effect**), in this case the effect explains 9% of the total variance

$r = .50$ (**large effect**), in this case the effect explains 25% of the total variance

The final thing needs to be mentioned on effect size is that when we are calculating the effect size, we do it from a given sample. When we looked at the means in a sample we see that we used them to draw inferences about the mean of the entire population. The same is true for effect size. That is, the size of effect in a population is the value in which we are interested, but since we have no access to this value, we use the effect size in the sample to estimate the likely size of the effect in the population.

Outliers

Sometimes in your data you will find points which stand out as being different from the bulk of the data. Those points are generally referred to as **outliers**. If we are using the mean, one outlier can have a large effect on describing the typical value of a data set. Outliers are very problematic for statistics (and by this we mean parametric statistical methods which do not use robust methods of estimation) because data are assumed to follow a normal distribution exactly. If you have a distribution that is approximately normal, this unfortunately does not result in approximately correct conclusions. If you are doing a complex math problem and you forget to carry a one to the tens position when adding numbers together, this will result in a completely wrong conclusion, not an approximately wrong conclusion. The presence of an outlier means that the distribution is not exactly a normal distribution.

One-tailed and two-tailed hypotheses

In the type of hypothesis testing we have just described, the default method of testing the hypothesis is to use a **two-tailed test**. Thus, if we have an alpha level of $a = .05$, this means that we would reject results that fell in the highest 2.5% of the distribution or the lowest 2.5% of the distribution, making up a total 5% probability that the data would be as extreme as or more extreme than what we found. In other words, in our null hypothesis, we would be examining both the possibility that the explicit group was better than the implicit group and the possibility that the explicit group was worse than the implicit group. The hypothesis could go in either direction. However, if the only thing we care about is just one of the possibilities, then we can use a one-tailed test. For example, let's say at the current moment we are already using the explicit way of practicing grammar in our classes. So we don't really care to know if the explicit way is better than the implicit way; we only want to know if the implicit way is better than the explicit one, because if it is we'll then implement that into our curriculum (in reality, we think we would want to know if the implicit method was worse, but, for purposes of illustrating what a one-tailed test is, let's just pretend we only care about one outcome). A **one-tailed** or **directional** test of a hypothesis looks only at one end of the distribution. A one-tailed test will have more power to find differences, because it can allocate the entire alpha level to one side of the distribution and not have to split it up between both ends.

Confidence Interval

Reporting confidence intervals, along with effect sizes, is something considered vital to improving researchers' intuitions about what statistical testing is. Reporting confidence intervals alongside (or in place of) p-values is recommended by many researchers, who point out that confidence intervals provide more information than p-values about effect size and are more useful for further testing comparisons (Kline, 2004; Maxwell & Delaney, 2004; Wilcox 2001, 2003; Wilkinson & Task Force, 1999). The **confidence interval** represents a range of plausible values for the corresponding parameter, whether that parameter is the true mean, the difference in scores, or whatever. With a 95% confidence interval, if the study were replicated 100 times, 95% of the time the parameter would be found within the confidence interval range. The p-value can show if the comparison found a significant difference between the groups, but the confidence interval shows how far from zero the difference lies, giving an intuitively understandable measure of effect size. In addition, the width of the confidence interval indicates the precision with which the difference can be calculated or, more precisely, the amount of sampling error. Higher power in a study will result in smaller confidence intervals and more precision in estimating correlations or mean differences in samples. If there is a lot of sampling error in a study, then confidence intervals will be wide, and we must say that our statistical results may not be very good estimates.

Having considered and discussed the most often used variables, the rest of the book will focus on more practical issues containing the variables.

Review questions
1. How do you define research in your own words?
2. What are the differences between one-tailed and two-tailed hypotheses? Provide examples.
3. Determine the kind of scale of measurement for each of the following variables.
   a) Weight   b) temperature   c) grammar scores   d) sex
   e) Years of school   f) age   g) level of proficiency   h) native language
4. Elaborate on effect size.

5. What is confidence interval? When should it be taken into account?

CHAPTER TWO

Familiarity with different parts of SPSS

What is SPSS?

SPSS is a comprehensive and flexible statistical analysis and data management system. SPSS is available from several platforms such as Windows, Macintosh, and the UNIX systems. SPSS for windows has the advantage of bringing the full power of the mainframe version of SPSS to the personal computer environment. It makes you able to perform many analyses on your PC that were once possible only on much larger machines. Here in this chapter, you will become familiar with the basic sections of SPSS.

How to start SPSS?

There are three different ways by which an SPSS program can be run:

- To spot the SPSS icon on your PC and then put your cursor on it and double-click.
- From the **start** menu on your windows, select **All programs**. Then using your cursor, point to SPSS for windows and click on the SPSS program (figure 2-1).
- SPSS also will start if you double-click on an SPSS data file listed in windows explorer.

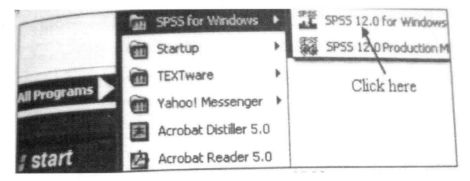

Figure 2-1. Starting SPSS

SPSS windows

There are five main types of window for SPSS programs. They are briefly explained below.

1- Data editor window

When you start an SPSS program, the first window which appears on your PC screen is data editor window. This window allows you to enter your data into the SPSS program to be analyzed. Different actions like opening and closing existing data files, creating new files, entering our data, making changes to the existing data files, and also running different statistical analyses can be achieved in this window. The last point is that the editor windows are saved with .sav extensions. Figure 2-2 is a sample of editor window.

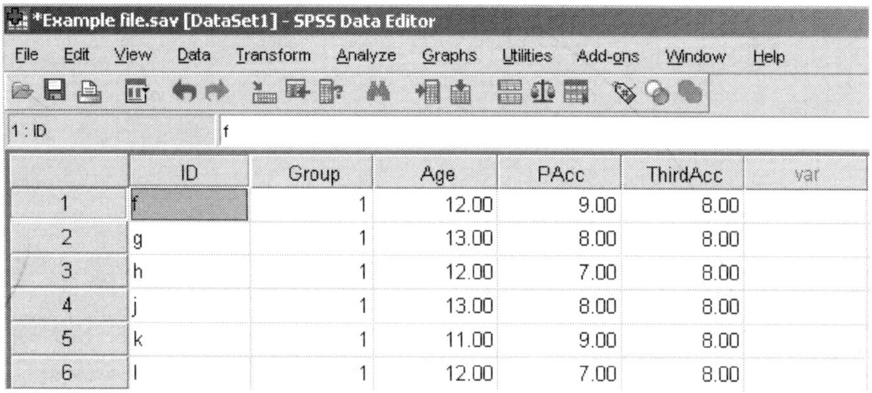
*Example file.sav [DataSet1] - SPSS Data Editor
File Edit View Data Transform Analyze Graphs Utilities Add-ons Window Help
1 : ID
f
ID Group Age PAcc ThirdAcc var
1 f 1 12.00 9.00 8.00
2 g 1 13.00 8.00 8.00
3 h 1 12.00 7.00 8.00
4 j 1 13.00 8.00 8.00
5 k 1 11.00 9.00 8.00
6 l 1 12.00 7.00 8.00

Figure 2-2 Data editor window

As it is clear from the figure, data editor window consists of two parts: **Data view** and **Variable view** (at the bottom left corner). Data view is used to enter the data. Each column is used for one type of data. When you enter your data in the first column, the computer assumes it as a variable and names it as VAR00001 unless you give it a name in the variable view. That is, one can not enter the name of a variable directly on the data view. Rather, it must be done in the variable view.

However, when you want to work in the variable view part, there should be regarded some specifications. First, you can not start the name of your data with number. That is, first you should use letter and then you can use numbers as you wish. Second, spaces are not allowed in the variable view part. In other words, if you use a space, the computer warns you and will not permit you to use it by showing a warning window (see figure 2-3).

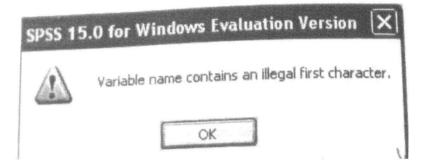

Figure 2-3 Warning window

Another part of the variable view is the **type** part. This part allows you to select the kind of data you want to enter. That is, if you want to enter numbers you need to select the **Numeric** choice in this column. And if you want to enter names, the **String** choice must be chosen.

2- Viewer window

This window makes it possible for you to see the output tables or sometimes-called pivot tables resulted from running a specific statistical analysis. When you run a specific statistical analysis on your data, the viewer window will open automatically. When you have a viewer window, you can do some actions like modifying the output tables, copying them, deleting them, or even transferring them into a Word document. The point needs to be mentioned is that a viewer screen consists of two main parts: on the left-side of the screen is an outline or menu showing a full list of all the analyses you have conducted. On the right-side of the screen are the results of your analyses which may include tables and charts. Viewer windows are saved with .spo extensions. Figure 2-4 represents a sample of viewer window.

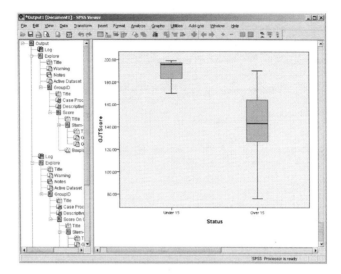

Figure 2-4 Viewer window

3- Pivot table editor window

This is a window which appears in the viewer window and is used to make changes in font, size, dimensions of columns, and on the whole, the appearance of the pivot tables. To appear and use the pivot table editor window, you just need to double-click on the specific table(s) you want to modify.

4- Chart editor window

This type of window is the same as pivot table editor window. The difference is that while the pivot table editor window is used to make changes in the appearance of output tables, the chart editor window is used to do the same things in the graphs or charts presented in the viewer window. Like the pivot table editor window, by just double-clicking on the chart(s) the chart editor window will appear. Figure 2-5 is a sample of chart editor window.

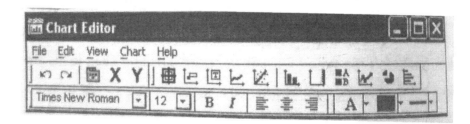

Figure 2-5 chart editor

Syntax editor window

This window is used when it is tried to repeat a lot of analyses or generate a number of similar graphs. It allows you to copy and paste commands, and to make modifications to the commands generated by SPSS. The results of this window are stored in a separate text file with a .sps extension. The important point is that the commands pasted to the syntax editor don't function until you select to run them. To do so, you need first to highlight the specific command (even the last full stop) and then click on the **Run** button or on the arrow icon in the menu bar.

Sorting the data

If you desire to arrange the names you entered in the editor window, just select **sort** from the **Data** menu. Doing so, a dialogue box opens (see figure 2-6). You should now indicate the variable you want to sort. Then you should decide whether you want to sort the selected data in a descending or ascending order by clicking on the respective button.

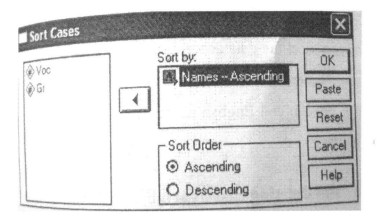

Figure 2-6 Sorting window

Inserting and deleting cases/variables

If you want to add a variable or case in the middle of variables and cases, you just need to use either the **Data view** or **Variable view,** but notice that cases can be inserted in the Data view only. Here we use just the Data view for both. To insert a variable, put your cursor in the column to the left of which you want to add a variable. Then from the Data menu in the toolbar select **Insert Variable** or simply click the **Insert Variable** button. To add a case, again put you cursor on the row above which you wish to add a case. Then select **Insert case** in the **Edit** menu. Or just simply click on the

Insert case option.

To delete a variable, select the whole column (by clicking on the variable name) and then press the **delete** key on your keyboard. To delete a case, click on the case number in the left column and press the **delete** key.

Computation

SPSS also allows you make computations. To do so, select **Compute** from the **Transform** menu. In the box appears, write the name of new variable under the **Target variable.** In the **Numeric expression,** type the formula of your calculation using either the keys available in the box or your own computer keys (figure 2-7).

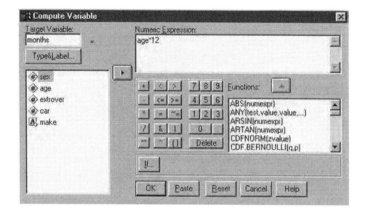

Figure 2-7 computation window

Closing SPSS program

Having entered our data and analyzed them, when you want to close the program, just click on the **File** menu at the top left of the screen. Click on **Exit**. SPSS will prompt you to save your data file and the file containing your output.

Review questions

1. What is SPSS? What are its uses?
2. What are the five main windows of SPSS? Elaborate on them.
3. What is the purpose of Syntax editor window?
4. What steps need to be taken in order to be able to do a computation in SPSS?
5. Is it possible to make any changes in the tables appeared in the viewer window? If yes, how?

CHAPTER THREE

Descriptive statistics

Preliminaries

While it may be tempting to start looking at relationships between variables straight away, it is a good idea to look at our individual variables first. We usually need to know how our respondents have replied to particular questions or how many times a teacher has asked a particular question, for example, before we can go and look at relationships with other variables. We might often just want to know how many boys and girls are in our sample. This kind of descriptive information can give us useful information on our variables and our research questions. Because we are looking at individual variables, this type of analysis is called *Univariate analysis*. As well as providing important information, Univariate analysis can help us to look out for mistakes that may have been made during data input. We can spot some (but obviously not all) errors by seeing whether there are values which are outside of the range of possible values (for example, if we have coded boys as 1 and girls as 2, we wouldn't expect to find any 3s!).

Descriptive statistics

Descriptive statistics are just employed to summarize or better to say describe a group of data. In other words, they can be helpful in that they enable us to see what kind of data we have, and how they have been distributed. There are two main types of descriptive statistics: Measures of central tendency and Measures of variability. They are first illuminated below and then the way we can obtain them through SPSS will be presented.

Measures of central tendency

These kinds of descriptive statistics are used to show the most typical behavior of a group. **Mode**, **Median**, and **Mean** are the three most widely used kinds of measures of central tendency.

Mode

Mode is the simplest type of measures of central tendency to obtain and is simply the most common value in a group. It is the score that is obtained by the individuals more than other scores. As an example, in the following set of scores, 14 is considered to be the mode.

17, 13, 12, 14, 10, 14, 14, 20, 18, 17

However, there are some cases in which there are two modes (known as bimodal distributions), three modes (as trimodal distributions), or even no mode at all (flat distributions). To be able to show the mode in graphs, it is the base line in the polygon and the highest bar in the bar graph and also histogram.

The main problem with mode is that it is very sensitive to chance scores. For example, in the following example, mode is 60.

35, 35, 40, 40, 45, 45, 45, 46, 46, 48, 52, 55, 60, 60, 60, 60, 65, 70

However, if one of the students whose score is 46, just by chance scores 45 and one of the students who scored 60 had scored 61 instead, the mode would shift from 60 to 45. Of course, notice that this problem of mode decreases, as the number of students increases.

Median

Median is essentially the middle value in a distribution. We can find that by ordering our values from the lowest to the highest, and then seeing which one the middle one is. In the following set of data, for instance, the median is 29 because it is the midpoint of the set.

50, 48, 48, 47, 42, 41, 36, 31, 29, 28, 24, 22, 21, 19, 18, 16, 15

However, if the number of data is even, the two middle scores should be added and then divided by two in order to get the median. For example, the median of the following points is 16.5.

20, 18, 17, 17, 17, 16, 15, 12, 10, 7

Mean

Usually, when we speak about average in every day terms, the value we are thinking of is the *mean*. The mean is simply *the sum of the values of all the cases divided by the total number of cases*. It is, in fact, the most common type of measures of central tendency and is also thought of as an arithmetic point. By arithmetic point it means that if the scores are distributed along a continuum, the mean will be exactly at the balance point.

Measures of variability

These kinds of descriptive statistics provide information as to the dispersion of scores around the mean. **Range**, **Standard deviation**, and **Variance** are three common types of measures of central tendency.

Range

The first way of looking at spread seems obvious. Just subtract the lowest score from the highest score to get the *range* of values in your dataset. As an instance, in the following group of scores, the range is 13.

10, 12, 7, 8, 18, 20, 19, 14, 18, 19, 20

Range is the simplest type of measures of variability to obtain; but since it is sensitive to extreme scores, it is not very reliable.

Standard deviation

The most reliable type of measures of variability is standard deviation (SD). It is a measure of the extent to which the values in a distribution cluster around the mean. That is, it not only takes into account all the scores, but it accounts for the average differences of the scores from the mean.

Variance

Variance is another type of measures of dispersion and is simply a measure of variability of data. It is related to SD closely. In fact, the standard deviation equals the square root of the variance. The variance in turn is the sum of the squared deviations of the observations from their mean divided by the number of observations minus 1.

Descriptive statistics in SPSS

In order to obtain the descriptive statistics of your data, you just suffice to take the following steps:
- Once we have opened the file and entered our data, we will need to go to the button marked **Analyze** because this is where all are statistical analyses are to be found.

- When we click that button, a new box pops up. This lists a whole slew of statistical procedures. We want to choose **Descriptive Statistics** because at this stage we are just going to describe our variable.
- When we click this, a new box comes up with a new list of choices. We choose **Descriptives** (See Figure 3-1).

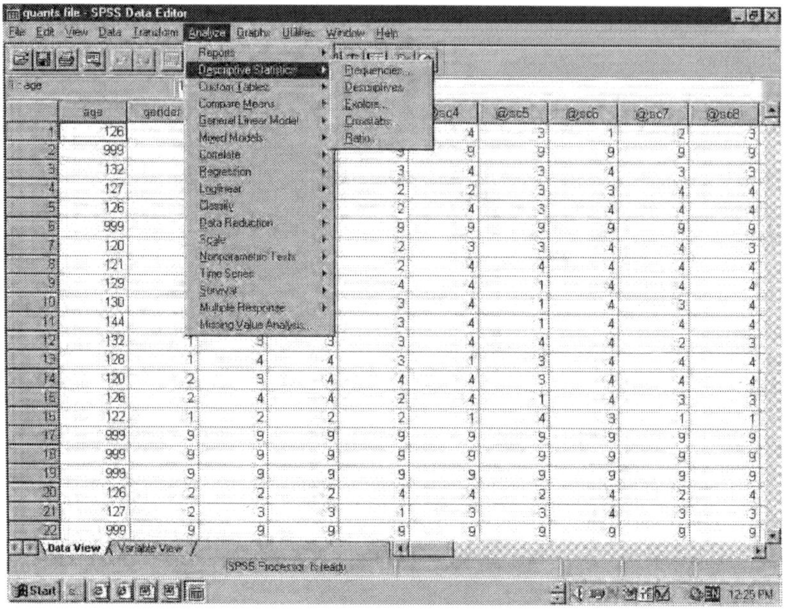

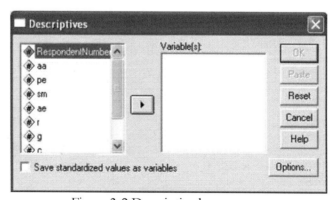

Figure 3-1 Producing a descriptive Table

- After selecting **Descriptives**, a new window opens. Here you should move the variables whose statistics you wish to get into the **Variable(s)** box. We do this by clicking the arrow in the middle. The variable then jumps to the right-hand box. (See figure 3-2).

Figure 3-2 Descriptive box

20

- There is also an **Options** button at the right hand corner in the bottom. A click on this button will show a dialogue box, like Figure 3.3, where you can make the choices you need. In this box there are both circles and squares. With circles you can choose just one choice at a time, but squares don't have any limitations. You can select as many as you desire.

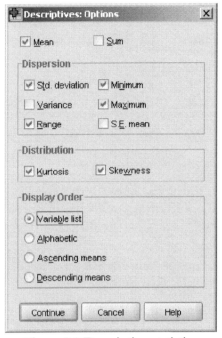

Figure 3.3 Descriptive statistics

- Having selected the choices you need (by ticking the small box next to them), click **Continue** and then **Ok**

Doing all these steps, the output tables representing the descriptive statistics of your data will be appeared in the viewer window. There are two main sections to this output (this will usually be the case in SPSS). The first box gives us some general information: the name of the variable, how many respondents actually answered the question and how many did not. The second box gives us our actual descriptives.

Frequency distribution

The first things we want to look at, while dealing with some data, is often things like how many people have answered in a certain way or how many respondents belong to different groups. The best way to do this is by looking at what we call a *frequency distribution* of the variable. In other words, frequency distribution represents data in a given order and implies how many times an item has been repeated in the data. To obtain frequency data in SPSS, like what we did for Descriptive statistics, from button **Analyze** we select **Descriptives statistics**. Then, here we choose **Frequencies** choice.

Like the previous case, now we should move our desirable variables into the new box appeared (See Figure 3.4).

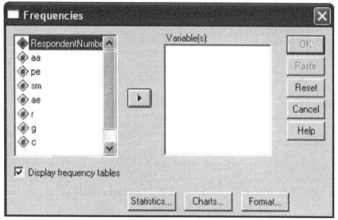

Figure 3-4 Frequency box

Then there is a button named **statistics**. By clicking on it, a new dialogue box appears from which we can tick the choices we wish. Finally, in the last stage, we click on **continue** and then **Ok** (Figure 3.5).

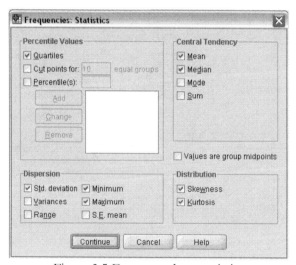

Figure 3.5 Frequency box statistics

In the output window, there will appear two main tables. The first one gives us some general information such as the name of the variable, how many respondents actually answered the question and how many did not answer the questions. The second box gives us our actual frequencies (See Figure 3.6).

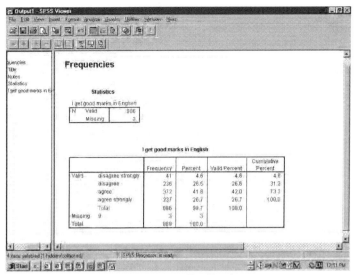

Figure 3.6 Frequency distribution outputs

Review questions

1. What is the use of descriptive statistics?

2. Provide mean, mode, and median of the following data.

1, 24, 24, 12, 18, 14, 23, 43, 25, 12, 11, 19, 20, 20, 34, 27, 37, 35, 19, 24, 42, 24

3. How is it possible to run the frequency distribution in SPSS?

4. What is the advantage of standard deviation over variance?

5. Enter the following data into your SPSS and then obtain all the descriptive statistics discussed in the chapter.

12, 13, 23, 17, 17, 14, 16, 18, 19, 20, 23, 21, 15, 15, 16, 17, 16, 13, 11, 10, 9, 14, 19, 20, 21, 12, 17, 17, 15, 16, 16, 17, 14, 13, 17, 17, 23, 32, 17, 22, 21, 13, 18, 18, 19, 14, 11, 10, 11, 18, 17, 18, 20, 20, 13, 21, 12, 17, 14, 16, 17, 18, 18, 18, 14, 19, 19, 20, 20, 13, 21, 22

6. The ages of students enrolled in one school in Shahrekord are: 21, 28, 42, 21, 21, 20, 19, 18, 33, 41, 37, 22, 23, 26, 26, 41, 42, 21, 21, 36, 21, 21, 24, 25, 22, 36, 21, 23. Find the mean, mode, and median for age.

7. Here are the scores of the first exam you gave in an introductory linguistics class. What are the mean, mode, median, and standard deviation? 88, 66, 34, 48, 88, 69, 99, 87, 88, 76, 89, 89, 68, 88, 89, 90.

CHAPTER FOUR
Graphs in SPSS

SPSS Graphs

In the preceding chapter, the ways the descriptive information and also the frequency distribution of data can be obtained were explained. Although it could yield valuable information, sometimes dealing with graphically-presented data can be more easily comprehensible. In this chapter, the main graphs accessible in SPSS (version 15) will be explained and the way they can be provided for a set of data is also elucidated.

Among different types of graphs which are available in SPSS (some of them are completely for technical purposes), the five ones that are mostly employed in social sciences are:

- Bar graph
- Histogram
- Line graph
- Scatter plot
- Pie graph

Bar graph

Bar graph is a kind of graph consisting of two axes: a horizontal line (called abscissa or x-axis) and a vertical line (called ordinate or y-axis). On the x-axis the scores or data and on the y-axis the frequency of data are presented. In order to gain a bar graph, two types of variables, a categorical and a continuous, are needed. That is, it can show the number of cases in specific categories. In order to gain a bar graph through SPSS, the following steps need to be taken:

- From the menu select the choice **Graphs**. And then select **Legacy Dialogs** (Legacy Dialogs allows us to choose the type of graph we wish). Figure 4.1 appears.

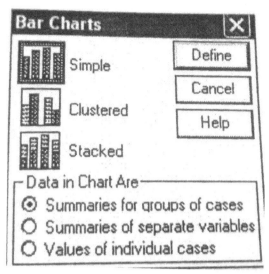

Figure 4.1 Bar Graph

- Having chosen the suitable kind of graph (**Bar**), click on the **Define** button. In the next opened window (figure 4.2), move your variable name into the box named **Category axis**.

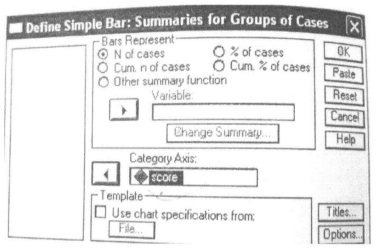

Figure 4.2 Define Simple Bar Graph

- Then to determine what data should be shown on the y-axis, the desired case (usually the number of cases) is moved to the variable box. Then click **OK**. Figure 4.3 is a sample of a bar graph.

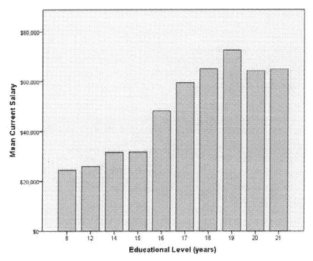

Figure 4.3 Bar graph sample

Histogram

A histogram of a frequency distribution is created by assigning score values to the horizontal line, putting potential frequency values on the vertical line, and marking an asterisk or "X" to show each case that receives a score. Histograms represent the distribution of a single continuous variable. To obtain a histogram in SPSS, like the bar graph, first you should click on **Graphs** from menu and then on **Legacy Dialogs**. After defining and moving the desired variable into the appropriate box, click on **OK**.

Line graph

The format of line graph is also the same as the two preceding ones. However, in the line graph instead of a bar, a line shows the frequency distribution of data. Moreover, it makes it possible for us to investigate the mean score of a continuous variable along a number of values of a categorical variable. Like the previous cases, to obtain a line graph in SPSS, we select **Graphs** from menu. After choosing **Legacy Dialogs**, we define and move our variable into the appropriate box. Then click **OK**. A sample of line graph is available in figure 4.4.

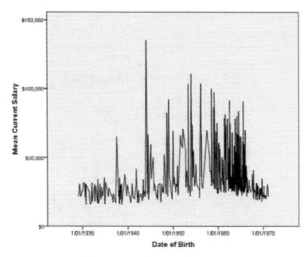

Figure 4.4 Line graph Sample

Scatter plot

Scatter plot is one kind of diagram reflecting the direction and the degree of relationship between two continuous types of data. It is usually taken into account before calculating the degree of correlation between the variables. To reach a scatter plot in SPSS, again we select the **Graphs** from the menu. After clicking on **Legacy Dialogs** and defining the type of graph, we move the dependent and independent variables into **Y-axis** and **X-axis** boxes respectively. Then click on **OK** button (Figure 4.5).

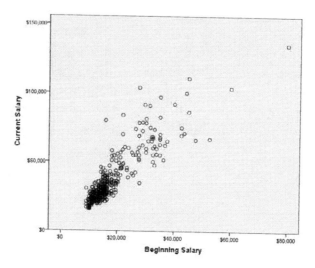

Figure 4.5 Scatter plot

Pie graph

Another type of graph which may be used (of course very rarely) is called pie graph. This kind of graph, a sample of which is Figure 4.6, can also be used to sow graphically the frequency of a set of scores. By clicking the **Graphs** button from the menu and the selecting **Legacy Dialogs** and **Pie** respectively, a window like Figure 4.7 appears. Here again we define and choose the type of pie graph like the previous cases and lastly click **OK**.

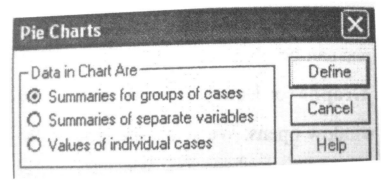

Figure 4.6 Pie graph window

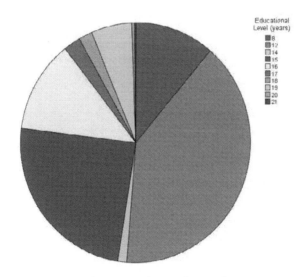

Figure 4.7 Pie graph sample

Editing the Graphs

After obtaining the desired graphs, you may feel to do some modifications on them. You may want to change the size, color, label, or the font of your graph. All these actions will be possible by just double clicking on the graph. Doing so, the Chart Editor window appears (Figure 2.5 is a sample of chart editor window). Using this Table, you can make different changes in your graph. To do so, you just suffice to click on the appropriate button and then make the changes you wish. Figure 4.8 is a brief description of the main buttons in the chart editor window.

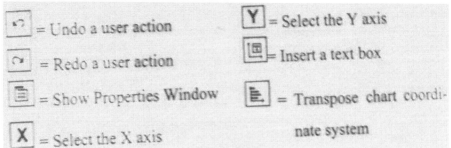

Figure 4.8 Chart Editor Buttons

When you have done all your modifications in the viewer window, it is time to import it into your Microsoft word document. To do it, just right click on the graph and click the **Copy** button. Then go to your word document and put your cursor in the appropriate space you want the graph to be presented. Then again right click that space and click the **Paste** button. In this way, the graph will be presented in your word document.

Review questions
1. How can we run SPSS to obtain a specific kind of graph?
2. How is it possible to make changes in the graphs obtained?
3. Consider the following data.

Gender	Speaking score	Writing score	Reading score
1	18	17	19
2	13	14	18
2	20	13	19
1	17	16	18
2	13	15	20
2	16	16	17
1	16	16	18
1	15	17	16
1	15	16	17
2	16	13	18

2	19	19	19
2	18	17	20
1	18	16	15
1	14	15	19
1	18	16	17

a) Obtain the bar graph between Gender and reading scores
b) Obtain the pie graph for reading and speaking score?
c) Obtain the histogram for writing scores?
d) Obtain the bar graph, histogram, and pie graph for reading score.

CHAPTER FIVE
T-test: Comparing two means

Preliminaries: T-test and its types

The **t-test** is the simplest test of whether groups differ. Even if we tested two populations that we thought were exactly the same, there would be some variation in scores among the groups. Therefore, the t-test determines if the differences between groups are small enough to attribute them to the random variation in scores that would happen each time we take a new sample of the same population, or whether the differences are large enough for the two groups to be thought of as belonging to two different populations. In other Words, frequently, we are interested in figuring out whether or not two groups have the same mean on some variable. We are interested in the question, "Did males and females in a specific study have similar mean academic ability scores?" To test the hypothesis of equality of means for two groups, we can use the *t-test* statistic.

However, there are two types of t-tests each of which appropriate for specific situations. One is called the **independent-samples t-test,** used when there are two different experimental conditions and different participants are assigned to each condition (it is also called independent measures); and the other is the **paired-samples t-test** which is utilized when there are two different experimental conditions but the same participants are assigned to the two conditions (sometimes referred to as matched-pairs).

Assumptions of T-test

There are four main assumptions (the violation of which may lead us to inaccurate results) for both types of t-tests:

1. The dependent variable should be measured in interval-level measurements.
2. The data should be independent.
3. The data should be normally distributed.
4. Groups should have equal variances.

The first two assumptions are covered well in most books about general research design (Hatch & Lazaraton, 1991; Mackey & Gass, 2005; Porte, 2002) and will not be discussed further in this chapter. The last two assumptions are ones that can be examined through the use of statistical software.

33

Although there are statistical tests to check for both the normality of your data and equal variances, Wilcox (2003) notes that a basic problem with such tests is that these tests "do not always have enough power to detect situations where the assumption should be discarded" (p. 241). He, in fact, does not recommend using them.

The assumption of equal variances is very often violated in second language research studies if a group of native speakers versus non-native speakers is included, since the native speakers usually have a far smaller variance than the group of non-native speakers. Fortunately, for t-tests there are estimators that can take unequal variances into account.

Independent T-test

An independent-samples t-test has the following attributes:

• It has exactly two variables.

• One variable is categorical with only two levels and it is the independent variable.

• The other variable is continuous and it is the dependent variable.

• If you took averages of the variables, you would have only two averages.

To perform an independent-samples t-test, go to **analyze** > **compare means** > **independent sample t-test** (see Figure 5.1). In the dialogue box, move your dependent variable into the "Test Variable(s)" box. Move the categorical grouping variable (independent variable) into the "Grouping Variable" box. You should then be able to click on the **define groups** button. If you can't, just click on your categorical variable to get it to highlight, and then the button should work. The reason you have to define groups in the "Independent Samples T-Test" dialogue box is that you may want to perform t-tests among different pairs of groupings. For example, if you had three different groups but decided to use t-tests to test them, you could do this by specifying that Group 1 = 1 and Group 2 = 2 the first time you run it, then Group 1 = 1 and Group 2 = 3 the second time you run it, and finally Group 1 = 2 and Group 2 = 3 the last time you run it.

Remember that in order to "Define groups" correctly you will need to use a variable with categories specified by numbers, not names (SPSS "strings"). If you have only strings you will need to recode your variable. It is, however, perfectly valid to have values for your numbered categorical variables. These can be entered in the "Variable View" tab, in the Values column. These will describe the variable while still keeping it classified as numerical in SPSS.

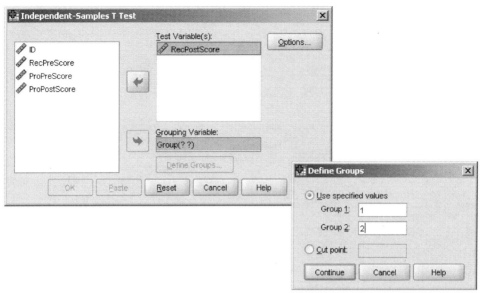

Figure 5.1. Independent T-test

There are two tables produced as the output to this test, and these are seen in Table 5.2. The first table, titled "**Group Statistics**," shows descriptive statistics. You should always check descriptive statistics first to get a sense of your data and make sure the N is correct. However, I have already commented on numerical summaries for this data so we will not look at this any further. The second table in the output is labeled "**Independent Samples Test**," and this table has the results of two different tests, and two columns labeled Sig. Be sure not to interpret the first significance level as the t-test! The first test is **Levene's test** for equality of variances. You can see that the Independent Samples Test table has two rows—one for a situation where you assume that variances are equal, and one when you assume they are not. The Levene's test for equality of variances will indicate whether you can use the line labeled "Equal variances assumed." If the **p-value** is greater than .05, you can use the first line; if not, use the second line. The output in Table 5.2 shows that the p-value for the Levene's test is p = .002, which means that the variances of the two groups are not equal. In this case, Levene's result lined up with our intuitions. You should also be aware that there can be problems of power in testing assumptions of parametric tests as the Levene's test does (Wilcox, 2003), so it may be safer to always use the second line with equal variances not assumed, which is also called **Welch's procedure**.

The result of the t-test for independent samples is found under the part of the table labeled "t-test for Equality of Means." However, we can get all of the important information out of the 95% CI for the difference between groups. The CI, in this case, ranges from −4.37 to .42. This means that the actual difference in scores between the groups will lie, with 95% confidence, in this interval. Since zero is found in this confidence interval, we know that we should not reject the null hypothesis. We also see that the interval is wide and so we do not have a precise estimate of the mean difference between groups.

Group Statistics

	Group	N	Mean	Std. Deviation	Std. Error Mean
RecPostScore	Non Think Aloud	39	3.92	4.313	.691
	Think Aloud	38	6.89	6.044	.980

Independent Samples Test

		Levene's Test for Equality of Variances		t-test for Equality of Means					95% Confidence Interval of the Difference	
		F	Sig.	t	df	Sig. (2-tailed)	Mean Difference	Std. Error Difference	Lower	Upper
RecPostScore	Equal variances assumed	10.565	.002	-1.651	75	.103	-1.972	1.194	-4.350	.407
	Equal variances not assumed			-1.644	66.808	.105	-1.972	1.199	-4.365	.422

Figure 5.2. Output results of Independent t-test

Effect size

Having compared the mean differences of the two intended groups, we should make decision to reject or retain the null hypothesis. If we retain the null hypothesis no further calculation is needed. But when we decide to reject the null hypothesis, we should determine the magnitude of the difference between the means. This is done through effect size. Effect size, to put it clearly, shows the strength of the association or, as it was mentioned, the relative magnitude of the difference between the means of the two groups. Unfortunately, at this time SPSS does not calculate the effect size for independent samples t-tests. To calculate the effect size, the following formula is often used:

$$\text{Eta squared} = \frac{t^2}{t^2 + df}$$

Where:

Eta square = effect size

Paired-sample T-test

A paired-samples t-test is used when you want to compare two sets of scores obtained from the same group of participants at two different occasions. So the two mean scores cannot be independent of each other.

A paired-samples test has the following attributes:

• It has exactly two variables.

• One variable is categorical with only two levels and it is the independent variable.

• The other variable is continuous and it is the dependent variable.

• If you took averages of the variables, you would have only two averages.

To perform a paired-samples t-test, go to **analyze > compare means > paired-sample t-test**. You will see the dialogue box that is shown in Figure 5.3. Because the paired-samples test must have a pairing of variables, the first variable you click from the list of variables on the left will go into the area labeled "**Variable1**" and the second will go into the area labeled "**Variable2**" (in previous versions of SPSS you needed to hold down the Ctrl key to select two variables at once to move to the right; you don't need to do that now). Note that because we are comparing variables measured at two different times, and they are both in separate columns, we can do the paired-samples t-test in SPSS with no further modification to the data.

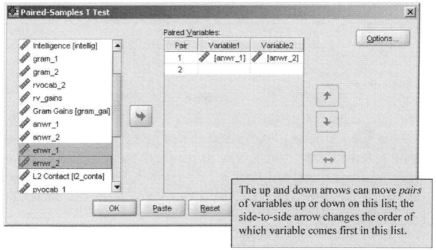

Figure 5.3. Paired-sample t-test

The output from this test is shown in Table 5.4. The first box of the output gives summary statistics (mean, standard deviation, sample size) which is not presented here. The second table of the output is labeled "Paired Samples Correlations" and shows the strength of the correlation between the two measures. Remember that the paired t-test assumes that the variables will be correlated, and that it could be problematic if they are not. You will want to examine the correlation assumption in this table, but don't be confused— this is not the t-test itself! Here we see there are very large correlations between both sets of variables. Notice that, if you have given the variable a label (usually longer and more descriptive than your variable name), it will be shown in the output as it is here.

The third table of the output contains the results of the paired-samples t-test. The first column is the mean difference between the two scores. If it is quite small in terms of the scale used, you would not expect to see a statistical difference for the t-test. If we just considered the p-value of $p = 0.07$, we might argue that we could reject the null hypothesis, that is there was no difference between measurements, but the CI argues for the differences being quite small. On the other hand, the differences between mean scores for Time 1 and Time 2 for the ENWR are larger.

Paired Samples Correlations

		N	Correlation	Sig.
Pair 1	Arabic Time 1 & Arabic Time 2	104	.985	.000
Pair 2	English Time 1 & English Time 2	104	.846	.000

Paired Samples Test

		Paired Differences							
					95% Confidence Interval of the Difference				
		Mean	Std. Deviation	Std. Error Mean	Lower	Upper	t	df	Sig. (2-tailed)
Pair 1	Arabic Time 1 - Arabic Time 2	-.250	1.392	.136	-.521	.021	-1.832	103	.070
Pair 2	English Time 1 - English Time 2	-3.106	2.216	.217	-3.537	-2.675	-14.292	103	.000

Figure 5.4. Output results of paired-t-test

Review questions

1. What is t-test? What are its two types? When can they be used?

2. An M.A student of Shiraz University is to investigate the influence of Persian and English glossing on the reading scores of Persian EFL language learners. She selects two different groups of learners. Then, she provides Persian glossing for one class and English gloss for the other group of learners. The following data were obtained. What type of t-test is suitable for her to run? Why? You run the appropriate program and report the results.

Persian glossing group	English glossing group
23	22
27	26
26	17
25	19
29	27
27	26
15	24
15	18
18	17
17	15
30	14
28	19
26	21
18	17

3. A researcher is going to see whether is there any difference in the performance of students in the morning and at night or not. To get an answer, he selected a class and required them to take a test twice. In the first administration, they took the test in the morning, and in the second one (with a 15-day time log), they sat for the test at night. The following data were gathered. In order to

analyze the data, what statistical program is suitable? Why? You run the intended program and report the results.

Morning scores	Night scores
19	15
20	15
17	14
16	19
18	15
17	13
15	11
15	16
20	17
15	17
19	14
16	14
20	20
18	17

CHAPTER SIX
ANOVA: Comparing multiple means
Preliminaries

In the preceding chapter, we talked about how we could make a comparison between two means obtained from two conditions or groups. The tests discussed in that chapter were, however, limited to two levels of independent variables (i.e. two experimental groups). There are, however, cases in which there are more than two levels of independent variables. In these situations, a new statistical analysis approach referred to as analysis of variance (ANOVA) is appropriate.

ANOVA

As it was above-mentioned, ANOVA has the advantage of making it possible to make a comparison among a set of means. ANOVA is an acronym for Analysis of Variance. A one-way ANOVA is the analysis of the variance of values (of a dependent variable) by comparing them against another set of values (the independent variable). It is a test of the hypothesis that the mean of the tested variable is equal to that of the factor. In other words, What ANOVA does is test the null hypothesis that several group means are equal in the population. You may wonder why the method is called analysis of variance when we want to compare the means. This is because ANOVA works by comparing the spread (or variance) of the group means (called the *between-groups sum of squares*) with the spread (or variance) of values within the groups (called the *within-group sum of squares*). It can be is used when you want to test whether the scores of three or more groups differ statistically.

A one-way ANOVA has the following attributes:

• It has exactly two variables.

• One variable is categorical with three or more levels and it is the independent variable.

• The other variable is continuous and it is the dependent variable.

• If you took averages of the variables, you would have three or more averages.

ANOVA is of different types: One-way ANOVA, Two-way ANOVA, Three-way ANOVA, etc. It depends on the number of independent variables. For example, if we have two independent variables two-way ANOVA should be used. If there is three independent variables three-way ANOVA is suitable and so on.

One-way ANOVA in SPSS

To obtain ANOVA in SPSS the following steps need to be taken:

First we choose **Analyze** from the menu, then the button **Compare means** is selected and finally **One-way ANOVA** should be clicked. Having taken these steps, a box like Figure 6-1 appears. In this dialogue box, you should enter the intended dependent variable into the **Dependent List** and the independent variable under **Factor** box.

Figure 6.1 One-way ANOVA window

Having done so, you should click **Post Hoc** button to make it possible to have two by two comparisons subsequently. In the Post Hoc window (Figure 6-2), the type of analysis may be selected. There are a set of options in this box. However, the two more widely used approaches are **Scheffe test** and **Tukey's test**. Finally click **Continue** and then **Ok**.

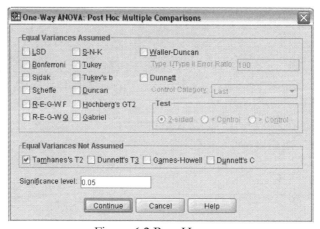

Figure 6.2 Post Hoc test

One-way ANOVA outputs

Running one-way ANOVA, two main output tables are obtained. The first one is ANOVA results table (Figure 6-3). In this table, the first thing which should be examined is the column labeled **Sig.** If the value in this column is smaller than .05 or .01, it can be concluded that there is a significant difference between the groups. Otherwise, the difference is not significant.

		Sum of Squares	df	Mean Square	F	Sig.
level of teaching	Between Groups	.522	3	.174	5.84	.001
	Within Groups	5.62	189	.030		
	Total	6.15	192			

Figure 6.3 ANOVA results output

In the table given, there is a significant difference between the groups of the study (Sig. = .001 < .05). However, we don't know which two groups are significantly different from each other. To be able to conclude on this, Post Hoc table can be a great help (Figure 6-4). At every point of this table that there is an asterisk (*) it can be inferred that there is a significant between those two groups. In the table below, as it is conspicuous, there is a significant difference between Lg.L and Lg.T groups.

Dependent Variable	(I) code	(J) code	Mean Difference (I-J)	Std. Error	Sig.	95% Confidence Interval Lower Bound	Upper Bound
level of teaching	lg.L	lg.T	-.070*	.026	.039	-.139	-.002
		N.I.expert	-.200*	.063	.009	-.364	-.037
		I.expert	-.160	.078	.177	-.365	.043
	lg.T	lg.L	.070*	.026	.039	.002	.139
		N.I.expert	-.130	.064	.185	-.299	.036
		I.expert	-.090	.079	.674	-.297	.117
	N.I.expert	lg.L	.200*	.063	.009	.037	.364
		lg.T	.130	.064	.185	-.036	.296
		I.expert	.040	.098	.977	-.215	.295
	I.expert	lg.L	.160	.078	.177	-.043	.365
		lg.T	.090	.079	.674	-.117	.297
		N.I.expert	-.040	.098	.977	-.295	.215

Figure 6.4 Post Hoc output

Effect size

Pallant (2005) asserts that in order to calculate the effect size in one-way ANOVA, the following formula can be used:

$$\text{Eta squared} = \frac{SSB}{SST}$$

Where

Eta squared = effect size

SSB= sum of squares between groups

SST = sum of squares total

Two-way ANOVA in SPSS

It was stated that two-way ANOVA is used when there are two independent variables in the study. To run two-way ANOVA these steps need to be taken in SPSS:

First select **General linear model** from **Analyze** menu. In the new window which pops up (Figure 6-5) select **Univariate**.

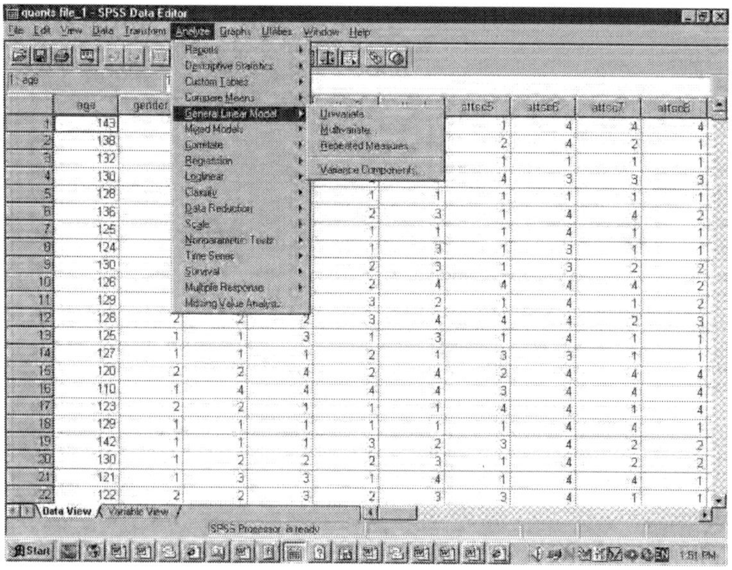

Figure 6.5 ANOVA window

In the new box that appeared, we specify our dependent and independent variables (Figure 6-6). The first thing we need to do is to choose our dependent variable. In the list of variables we select dependent variable and click on the arrow next to **Dependent**

44

to transfer it into Dependent box. Next, we need to choose our independent variable. In ANOVA, this is called the **Fixed Factor**. From the list of variables we choose independent variables and click on the arrow next to Fixed Factor(s). The variable now appears in that box.

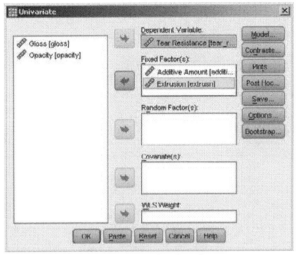

Figure 6.6 Univariate box

The next step to do is clicking on the **Post Hoc** button. In the newly opened window, we should move our independent variables into the **Post Hoc Tests** box. Finally, choosing the method of analysis (Scheffe or Tukey), click on **Continue** and **Ok** buttons.

Two-way ANOVA outputs

Two tables are presented in the output window. The first one represents the results of two-way ANOVA. In this table, the column Sig. should be examined. If its value is less than .05 or .01 (depending on our specified level of significance) it can be concluded that the difference between the groups is significant. If not, the difference is not significant. The point with regard to this table is that, unlike one-way ANOVA, this table also shows the interaction between the variables. That is, it reveals if the two independent variables mutually affect dependent variable or not (Figure 6-7).

Tests of Between-Subjects Effects

Dependent Variable:Tear Resistance

Source	Type III Sum of Squares	df	Mean Square	F	Sig.
Corrected Model	2.501ᵃ	3	.834	7.563	.002
Intercept	920.724	1	920.724	8351.243	.000
additive	.760	1	.760	6.890	.018
extrusn	1.740	1	1.740	15.787	.001
additive * extrusn	.000	1	.000	.005	.947
Error	1.764	16	.110		
Total	924.990	20			
Corrected Total	4.265	19			

a.R Squared = .506 (Adjusted R Squared = .509)

Figure 6.7 Results of two-way ANOVA

The second table presented in the output window is referred to as Post Hoc results (Figure 6.8). As it was already said for one-way ANOVA, this table pinpoints where exactly the difference between groups lies.

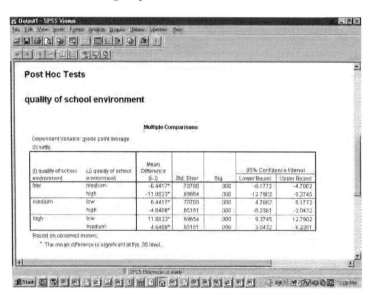

Figure 6.8 Post Hoc results test

Effect size

In two-way ANOVA, it is possible to calculate the effect size from the SPSS. To do so, when the Univariate box is opened (Figure 6-6), click on **Options** and in the newly opened box, go to the **Display** part and simply tick **Estimate of effect size**.

Review questions

1. What is ANOVA used for? How does it differ from t-test?
2. Is there any difference between the calculation of effect size in ANOVA and t-test?
3. Foreign students in an English class were asked to rate the short stories that they read during the course. Each story had a particular theme which you felt might influence their "appreciation" ratings. Here are the data:

Students	Story 1	Story 2	Story 3	Story 4
1	4	4	3	6
2	3	4	5	7
3	5	3	4	8
4	5	3	5	6
5	4	4	4	7
6	3	3	5	7

a) Find the mean for each group.
b) What statistical program is appropriate to see whether there is any significant relationship between the story themes and the appreciation ratings of students? Why?
c) Do the analysis and report the findings.

CHAPTER SEVEN

Correlation

Preliminaries

The test which is to be elaborated on in the current chapter is referred to as correlation. It looks at how two measurements go together; how they are related to each other. The meaning of correlation in a statistical sense is very much related to the meaning you would think of in ordinary life; you might notice that people in your neighborhood seem to wear heavy coats more in the winter than in the summer. If there is a relationship between type of coat and weather, there is a correlation between the two variables, and this means there is some kind of discernible linear pattern among the data. A test of correlation is thus looking for a pattern of relationships among data.

Correlation

Correlation analysis is, as it was above-cited, used to describe the degree and direction of the relationship between two variables. For instance, a researcher wants to know whether there is a relationship between language learners' reading comprehension ability and their repertoire of cognitive strategies. The degree of relationship is measured and represented by the **coefficient of correlation** –a value which can range between -1 and +1. The more distant the correlation coefficient from zero, the stronger the degree of the relationship between the two variables will be. Thus, while a correlation coefficient of zero indicates no relationship between the variables, correlation coefficients -1 and +1 represent perfect relationships (although their differ in the direction of the relationship: the direction of the relationship is negative if the obtained correlation coefficient is less than zero. However, in case the value is greater than zero, the direction of the relationship is positive).

Depending on the nature of the variables, you can use SPSS to measure either **Pearson Product Moment Correlation Coefficient (r)** or **Spearman Rank Order Correlation Coefficient (ϱ)**. Whereas the former procedure is used with interval variables, the latter is used when the two variables are ordinal.

Before jumping into the details of the procedures, it seems necessary to point out the assumptions underlying correlation analyses. In the event that any of these assumptions is violated, the correlation coefficient will be misrepresented. These assumptions are: *linearity, normality of distributions, and independence of observations.*

Linearity

The relationship between the two variables should be linear. To ascertain that this assumption is not violated, you should look at the scatterplot of the scores. It should show a roughly straight line, not a curve. To draw a scatterplot, from the menu at the top of the screen, click on *Graphs*, and then on *Scatter/Dot*. Click on *Simple Scatter* and then *Define*. Move one of the variables into the box marked *Y axis*, and the other one into the box labeled *X axis*. Now click on *OK* and you will have a Scatterplot like the one displayed here:

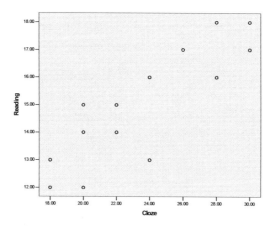

There appears to be a linear relationship between the two variables (i.e. Reading comprehension test and Cloze test) in this scatterplot. The data for this scatterplot are the data we will actually use for calculating Pearson correlation between the two variables. The linearity assumption, hence, is met here.

Normality of distributions

Scores on each variable should be normally distributed, i.e. they should not be skewed. This can be checked by examining the histograms of scores for each variable. To draw a histogram, from the menu on top of the screen, click on **Graphs**, and then on **Histogram** (fully illuminated in chapter 4). Move the variable of interest into the **Variables** box and click on **OK**. You will have graphs like the ones below if you use the data we will use in the example in the following section.

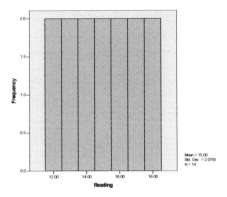

In this distribution, the frequencies of all scores are the same (i.e. two). The distribution, as a result, is flat, and not normal. This may distort the results of correlation.

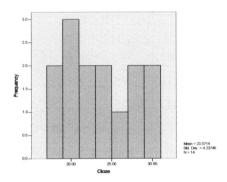

Although the distribution of Cloze scores is not flat, it is not normal either. Consequently, the normality assumption is violated. This means that correlation coefficient will probably not give us the precise picture of the relationship between the two variables. A noteworthy precaution, however, is that in reality we can not always anticipate that all the assumptions are fulfilled.

Independence of observations

The observations that make up your data must be independent of one another, i.e. each observation or measurement must not be influenced by any other observation or measurement. For instance, in studying the performance of students in pairs or small groups, the behavior of each member of the group influences all other group members, thereby violating the assumption of independence.

Procedure for Calculating Pearson r

To better understand the procedure, we will do it by considering an example. Suppose that a teacher wants to see if there is any relationship between language learners' reading ability and their performance on a cloze test in his class. The rational first step is to obtain the scores of a reading test and a close test. Suppose further that the following table represents the language learners' scores.

Students' Names	Reading Scores	Cloze Scores	Students' Names	Reading Scores	Cloze Scores
1. Lucy	18	28	8. Kathy	15	20
2. Jack	18	30	9. Nancy	14	20
3. David	17	30	10. Michael	14	22
4. Lisa	17	26	11. Abraham	13	24
5. Mat	16	28	12. Eli	13	18
6. Judith	16	24	13. Anthony	12	20
7. Aryan	15	22	14. Emily	12	18

After you open SPSS, in the Data View sheet, insert the reading scores under one column and the cloze scores under another column. Remember that you can label the column in the Variable View sheet. Now follow the instructions below to obtain Pearson r correlation coefficient:

1- From the menu at the top of the screen, click on **Analyze**, then click on **Correlate**, and then on **Bivariate**.

2- Select the two variables ad move them into the box marked **Variables**.

3- In the **Correlation Coefficient** section, the *Pearson* box is the default option. (In case we need to calculate Spearman ϱ correlation coefficient, we will have to tick the *Spearman rho* box).

4- Click on **OK**.

SPSS will give you a table like the following table:

Correlations

		Reading	Cloze
Reading	Pearson Correlation	1	.857**
	Sig. (2-tailed)		.000
	N	14	14
Cloze	Pearson Correlation	.857**	1
	Sig. (2-tailed)	.000	
	N	14	14

**. Correlation is significant at the 0.01 level

To interpret the output, you need to look at the value in front of Pearson Correlation in the table. In this case, the value is 0.857. There is no negative sign in front of this value. This means that there is a positive relationship between reading scores and close test performance. To determine the strength of relationship, you can adopt Cohen's (1998, pp. 79-81) suggestion:

small r= 0.10 to 0.29	medium r= 0.30 to 0.49	large r= 0.50 to 1.00

These guidelines apply whether or not there is a negative sign out the front of your r value. Remember, the negative sign refers only to the direction of the relationship, not its strength. The strength of correlations of r= 0.50 and r= -0.50 is the same. They only differ in direction.

Finally, you can report the results of the above example in this way: The relationship between language learners' reading ability and cloze test performance was investigated using Pearson product moment correlation coefficient. There was a strong positive relationship between the two variables, r= 0.85, n=14, p<0.01, with high levels of reading ability associated with high levels of performance on the cloze test.

Procedure for Calculating Spearman ϱ

This procedure is exactly the same as the procedure we used for calculating Pearson r, except that here our data, for one reason or another, exists in rank order. Let's do the analysis with the same example we had before. That is, we want to describe the relationship between reading ability and cloze test performance, but this time with ordinal data.

Students' Names	Reading Scores	Reading Rank	Cloze Scores	Cloze Rank	Students' Names	Reading Scores	Reading Rank	Cloze Scores	Cloze Rank
1. Lucy	18	1	29	3	8. Kathy	14.5	8	21	10
2. Jack	17.5	2	30	1	9. Nancy	14	9	20.5	11
3. David	17	3	29.5	2	10.Michael	13.5	10	23	8
4. Lisa	16.5	4	26	5	11.Abraham	13	11	24.5	6
5. Mat	16	5	28	4	12. Eli	12.5	12	17	13.5
6. Judith	15.5	6	24	7	13.Anthony	12	13	20	12
7. Aryan	15	7	22	9	14. Emily	11	14	17	13.5

After entering the data in the spreadsheet, we need to follow the same procedure we did for calculating Pearson Correlation Coefficient. The only difference here is that in Step 3, we need to tick **Spearman rho** box. Put differently, we need to click on **Analyze, Bivariate,** and **Correlate** respectively. Then we should move the variables into the box marked **variables**, tick **Spearman rho** box, and finally click on **OK**.

The output from the above-mentioned example is presented in the following table:

Correlations

			ReadingRank	ClozeRank
Spearman's rho	ReadingRank	Correlation Coefficient	1.000	.882**
		Sig. (2-tailed)	.	.000
		N	14	14
	ClozeRank	Correlation Coefficient	.882**	1.000
		Sig. (2-tailed)	.000	.
		N	14	14

**. Correlation is significant at the 0.01 level (2-tailed).

The value in front of Spearman rho is 0.882. No negative sign in front of this value indicates that there is a positive correlation between the two variables. The strength of the relationship can be determined by taking a look at Cohen's suggestion. That is, in this example, the relationship between the two variables is strong.

Reporting the results of Spearman rho correlation is quite similar to that of Pearson correlation: the relationship between language learners' reading ability and cloze test performance was investigated using Spearman rho correlation coefficient. There was a strong positive relationship between the two variables, r= 0.882, n=14, p<0.01, with high levels of reading ability associated with high levels of performance on the cloze test.

Calculating correlation between more than two variables

To calculate the relationship between more than two variables, we simply need to move all our variables into the **Variables** box and SPSS will provide us with correlations between each pair of variables. The procedure and the interpretation here are not different from the ones employed for calculating the correlation between two variables.

Review questions

1. What is the use of correlation?
2. What are the different uses of partial and multiple correlations?
3. What is the value of rho?
4. Draw a scatter gram of the following data and elaborate the graph.

Speed	88	120	100	98	111	121	87	127	110
Comprehension	20	48	55	50	30	44	45	20	30

CHAPTER EIGHT

Factor analysis

Introduction

Those who are social sciences students have certainly had situations in which they have had to measure a construct which is not directly measureable (often called a latent variable). Or they may have to develop a questionnaire and distribute it among the intended participants. However, the question is does every kind of questionnaire function adequately? Do not we have to check the reliability and validity of our instrument? There are certainly limitations on the development of an instrument like a questionnaire. In order to check the adequacy of instruments and also to measure unobservable constructs, one most-often used approach is Factor analysis which is to be discussed in this chapter.

Factor analysis

Factor analysis (or better to say exploratory factor analysis) is a statistical procedure and is in line with correlation. It attempts to identify underlying variables, or factors that explain the pattern of correlations within a set of observed variables. Factor analysis is often used in data reduction to identify a small number of factors that explain most of the variance that is observed in a much larger number of manifest variables. Factor analysis can also be used to generate hypotheses regarding causal mechanisms or to screen variables for subsequent analysis (for example, to identify collinearity prior to performing a linear regression analysis). Factor analysis has three main uses:

- To understand the structure of a set of variables.
- To construct a questionnaire to measure an underlying variable.
- To reduce a data set to a more manageable size while retaining as much of the original information as possible.

Factor analysis in SPSS

Having been assured about the suitability of your data, factor analysis can be run through taking the following steps: select **Data Reduction** from the **Analyze** menu and then click on the **Factor** choice. In the box that appears, select your intended variables and transfer them into the box labeled as Variable(s) (Figure 7-1).

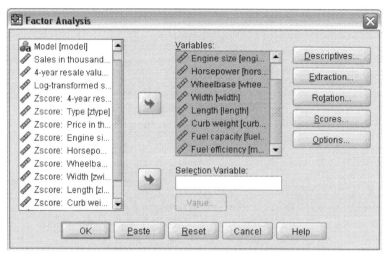

Figure 7.1 Factor analysis box

In the same box, you can choose your intended analyses like descriptive. To do so, you suffice to click on the intended button and then in the newly opened box, tick the appropriate choices. If you click the Descriptive button the following window appears (Figure 7-2). It contains choices such as:

Statistics: Univariate descriptives includes the mean, standard deviation, and number of valid cases for each variable. Initial solution displays initial communalities, eigenvalues, and the percentage of variance explained.

Correlation Matrix: The available options are coefficients, significance levels, determinant, KMO and Bartlett's test of sphericity, inverse, reproduced, and anti-image.

- **KMO and Bartlett's Test of Sphericity:** The Kaiser-Meyer-Olkin measure of sampling adequacy tests whether the partial correlations among variables are small. Bartlett's test of sphericity tests whether the correlation matrix is an identity matrix, which would indicate that the factor model is inappropriate.

- **Reproduced:** The estimated correlation matrix from the factor solution. Residuals (difference between estimated and observed correlations) are also displayed.

- **Anti-image:** The anti-image correlation matrix contains the negatives of the partial correlation coefficients, and the anti-image covariance matrix contains the negatives of the partial covariances. In a good factor model, most of the off-diagonal elements will be small. The measure of sampling adequacy for a variable is displayed on the diagonal of the anti-image correlation matrix.

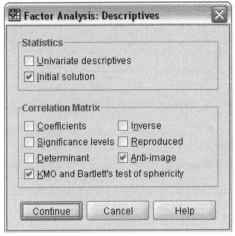

Figure 7.2 Descriptive box

Another option you can select in the factor analysis box is the **Extraction** button. By clicking on this button Extraction dialogue box pops up (Figure 7-3). Again in this window there are a set of options to choose. Different components of Extraction box are as follow:

Method: Allows you to specify the method of factor extraction. Available methods are principal components, unweighted least squares, generalized least squares, maximum likelihood, principal axis factoring, alpha factoring, and image factoring.

- **Principal Components Analysis:** A factor extraction method used to form uncorrelated linear combinations of the observed variables. The first component has maximum variance. Successive components explain progressively smaller portions of the variance and are all uncorrelated with each other. Principal components analysis is used to obtain the initial factor solution. It can be used when a correlation matrix is singular.

- **Unweighted Least-Squares Method:** A factor extraction method that minimizes the sum of the squared differences between the observed and reproduced correlation matrices (ignoring the diagonals).

- **Generalized Least-Squares Method:** A factor extraction method that minimizes the sum of the squared differences between the observed and reproduced correlation matrices. Correlations are weighted by the inverse of their uniqueness, so that variables with high uniqueness are given less weight than those with low uniqueness.

- **Maximum-Likelihood Method:** A factor extraction method that produces parameter estimates that are most likely to have produced the observed correlation matrix if the sample is from a multivariate normal distribution. The correlations are weighted by the inverse of the uniqueness of the variables, and an iterative algorithm is employed.

- **Principal Axis Factoring:** A method of extracting factors from the original correlation matrix, with squared multiple correlation coefficients placed in the diagonal as initial estimates of the communalities. These factor loadings are used to estimate new communalities that replace the old communality estimates in the diagonal. Iterations continue until the changes in the communalities from one iteration to the next satisfy the convergence criterion for extraction.

- **Alpha:** A factor extraction method that considers the variables in the analysis to be a sample from the universe of potential variables. This method maximizes the alpha reliability of the factors.

- **Image Factoring:** A factor extraction method developed by Guttman and based on image theory. The common part of the variable, called the partial image, is defined as its linear regression on remaining variables, rather than a function of hypothetical factors.

Analyze: Allows you to specify either a correlation matrix or a covariance matrix.

- **Correlation matrix:** Useful if variables in your analysis are measured on different scales.

- **Covariance matrix:** Useful when you want to apply your factor analysis to multiple groups with different variances for each variable.

Extract: You can either retain all factors whose eigenvalues exceed a specified value, or you can retain a specific number of factors.

Display: Allows you to request the unrotated factor solution and a scree plot of the eigenvalues.

- **Unrotated Factor Solution:** Displays unrotated factor loadings (factor pattern matrix), communalities, and eigenvalues for the factor solution.

- **Scree plot:** A plot of the variance that is associated with each factor. This plot is used to determine how many factors should be kept. Typically the plot shows a distinct break between the steep slope of the large factors and the gradual trailing of the rest.

Maximum Iterations for Convergence: Allows you to specify the maximum number of steps that the algorithm can take to estimate the solution.

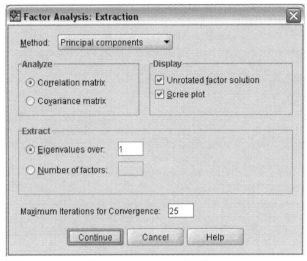

Figure 7.3 Extraction box

The third button in the factor analysis box is **Rotation** (Figure 7-4). Clicking on this button opens a new window consisting of the following choices:

Method: Allows you to select the method of factor rotation. Available methods are varimax, direct oblimin, quartimax, equamax, or promax.

- **Varimax Method:** An orthogonal rotation method that minimizes the number of variables that have high loadings on each factor. This method simplifies the interpretation of the factors.

- **Direct Oblimin Method:** A method for oblique (nonorthogonal) rotation. When delta equals 0 (the default), solutions are most oblique. As delta becomes more negative, the factors become less oblique. To override the default delta of 0, enter a number less than or equal to 0.8.

- **Quartimax Method:** A rotation method that minimizes the number of factors needed to explain each variable. This method simplifies the interpretation of the observed variables.

- **Equamax Method:** A rotation method that is a combination of the varimax method, which simplifies the factors, and the quartimax method, which simplifies the variables. The number of variables that load highly on a factor and the number of factors needed to explain a variable are minimized.

- **Promax Rotation:** An oblique rotation, which allows factors to be correlated. This rotation can be calculated more quickly than a direct oblimin rotation, so it is useful for large datasets.

Display: Allows you to include output on the rotated solution, as well as loading plots for the first two or three factors.

- **Rotated Solution:** A rotation method must be selected to obtain a rotated solution. For orthogonal rotations, the rotated pattern matrix and factor transformation matrix are displayed. For oblique rotations, the pattern, structure, and factor correlation matrices are displayed.
- **Factor Loading Plot:** Three-dimensional factor loading plot of the first three factors. For a two-factor solution, a two-dimensional plot is shown. The plot is not displayed if only one factor is extracted. Plots display rotated solutions if rotation is requested.

Maximum Iterations for Convergence: Allows you to specify the maximum number of steps that the algorithm can take to perform the rotation.

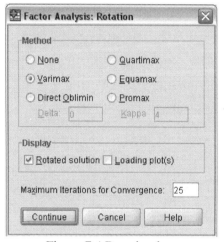

Figure 7.4 Rotation box

The penultimate button in the factor analysis window you can click is the **Scores** button. In so doing, a window like Figure 7.5 appears which comprises these sections:

Save as variables: Creates one new variable for each factor in the final solution.

Method: The alternative methods for calculating factor scores are regression, Bartlett, and Anderson-Rubin.

- **Regression Method:** A method for estimating factor score coefficients. The scores that are produced have a mean of 0 and a variance equals to the squared multiple correlation between the estimated factor scores and the true factor values. The scores may be correlated even when factors are orthogonal.
- **Bartlett Scores:** A method of estimating factor score coefficients. The scores that are produced have a mean of 0. The sum of squares of the unique factors over the range of variables is minimized.
- **Anderson-Rubin Method:** A method of estimating factor score coefficients; a modification of the Bartlett method which ensures orthogonality of the

estimated factors. The scores that are produced have a mean of 0, have a standard deviation of 1, and are uncorrelated.

Display factor score coefficient matrix: Shows the coefficients by which variables are multiplied to obtain factor scores. Also shows the correlations between factor scores.

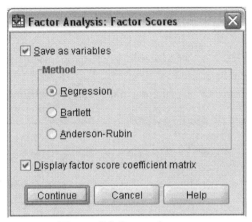

Figure 7.5 Scores button

Finally, the last button in the same box is the **Options** button (Figure 7-6) consisting of the following parts:

Missing Values: Allows you to specify how missing values are handled. The available choices are to exclude cases **listwise**, exclude cases **pairwise**, or replace with mean.

Coefficient Display Format: Allows you to control aspects of the output matrices. You sort coefficients by size and suppress coefficients with absolute values that are less than the specified value.

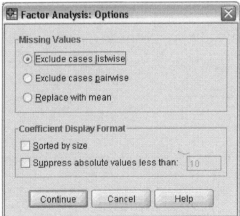

Figure 7.6 Options box

Factor analysis outputs

After going through all the above-cited steps, a host of output tables like **Correlation matrix, Inverse of correlation matrix, KMO and Bartlett's test, Anti image miracles, Scree plot**, etc. are shown all of which were explained in the preceding parts of the chapter.

Review questions

1. What are the three major uses of factor analysis?
2. When is it possible to run factor analysis? Can it be used for every data?
3. What steps do we need to take in order to run a factor analysis in SPSS?

CHAPTER NINE

Regression

Preliminaries

In the preceding chapters correlation and its applications were dealt with. Although correlation is a very useful research tool, it tells us nothing about the predictive power of the intended variables. This can be compensated for through regression, which is to be discussed in the present chapter. Linear Regression estimates the coefficients of the linear equation, involving one or more independent variables, which best predicts the value of the dependent variable. For example, you can try to predict a salesperson's total yearly sales (the dependent variable) from independent variables such as age, education, and years of experience.

Simple regression and multiple regression

When we want to **predict** or **account for** the variance in a dependent variable by means of variance in an independent variable, **Simple linear regression** is used. But if it is intended to do the same thing from more than one independent variable, Multiple regression is appropriate to use.

Regression in SPSS

To run regression in SPSS, having entered your data, you need to select **Regression** from **Analyze** menu and then click on **Linear**. Then in the appeared window (Figure 10.1) enter your dependent variable in the box labeled as **Dependent** and your independent variable(s) in to the **Independent**-labeled box.

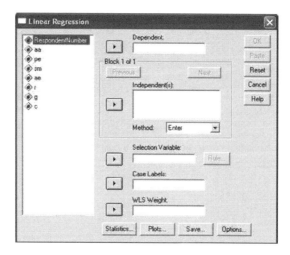

Figure 10.1 Linear regression box

In the same window just below the **Independent** box is **Method** choice. **Method** selection allows you to specify how independent variables are entered into the analysis. Using different methods, you can construct a variety of regression models from the same set of variables. Here different choices are briefly illuminated:

- **Enter (Regression):** A procedure for variable selection in which all variables in a block are entered in a single step.
- **Stepwise:** At each step, the independent variable not in the equation that has the smallest

  probability of F is entered, if that probability is sufficiently small. Variables already in   the regression equation are removed if their probability of F becomes sufficiently large.   The method terminates when no more variables are eligible for inclusion or removal.

- **Remove:** A procedure for variable selection in which all variables in a block are removed

  in a single step.
- **Backward Elimination:** A variable selection procedure in which all variables are entered into the equation and then sequentially removed. The variable with the smallest partial correlation with the dependent variable is considered first for removal. If it meets the criterion for elimination, it is removed. After the first variable is removed, the variable remaining in the equation with the smallest partial correlation is considered next. The procedure stops when there are no variables in the equation that satisfy the removal criteria.
- **Forward Selection:** A stepwise variable selection procedure in which variables are sequentially entered into the model. The first variable considered for entry

into the equation is the one with the largest positive or negative correlation with the dependent variable. This variable is entered into the equation only if it satisfies the criterion for entry. If the first variable is entered, the independent variable not in the equation that has the largest partial correlation is considered next. The procedure stops when there are no variables that meet the entry criterion.

There is also another choice in the same window labeled as **Statistics**. By choosing this button, a new box like Figure 10.2 appears in which you can tick **Descriptive**.

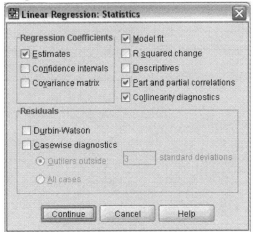

Figure 10.2 Regression statistics

Finally, to get the results, you should click **Continue** and **Ok** buttons. Of the five output tables provided by the SPSS, we are interested in three of them in regression analysis. The first one is the table named **Model summary** (Figure 10.3).

Model Summary[f]

Model	R	R Square	Adjusted R Square	Std. Error of the Estimate	Change Statistics				
					R Square Change	F Change	df1	df2	Sig. F Change
1	.335[a]	.112	.087	.43209	.112	4.422	1	35	.043
2	.582[b]	.339	.300	.37819	.227	11.686	1	34	.002
3	.683[c]	.467	.418	.34489	.127	7.884	1	33	.008
4	.688[d]	.473	.407	.34814	.006	.385	1	32	.539
5	.761[e]	.580	.512	.31585	.107	7.879	1	31	.009

a. Predictors: (Constant), NonVerbal Reasoning

b. Predictors: (Constant), NonVerbal Reasoning, Kinder L2 Reading Performance

c. Predictors: (Constant), NonVerbal Reasoning, Kinder L2 Reading Performance, Naming Speed

d. Predictors: (Constant), NonVerbal Reasoning, Kinder L2 Reading Performance, Naming Speed, Working Memory

e. Predictors: (Constant), NonVerbal Reasoning, Kinder L2 Reading Performance, Naming Speed, Working Memory, Phonological Awareness in L2

f. Dependent Variable: Grade1L1Reading Performance

Figure 10.3 Model summary

In this table the R squared column (also referred to as *multiple correlation* or *correlation of multiple determination*) should be considered. It is, in fact, the percent of the variance in the dependent variable explained, whether jointly or uniquely, by the independents.

The other table which is of interest in regression is the ANOVA table (Figure 10.4). The table indicates if the coefficient of multiple regression reported by R square is significant or not. To put it more clearly, it enables us to ensure that the independent variables significantly predict the variance in the dependent variable. To do so, just check the column titled as **Sig**. It should be less than p-value to be significant.

ANOVA[f]

Model		Sum of Squares	df	Mean Square	F	Sig.
1	Regression	.826	1	.826	4.422	.043[e]
	Residual	6.534	35	.187		
	Total	7.360	36			
2	Regression	2.497	2	1.248	8.729	.001[b]
	Residual	4.863	34	.143		
	Total	7.360	36			
3	Regression	3.435	3	1.145	9.625	.000[c]
	Residual	3.925	33	.119		
	Total	7.360	36			
4	Regression	3.481	4	.870	7.181	.000[d]
	Residual	3.879	32	.121		
	Total	7.360	36			
5	Regression	4.267	5	.853	8.555	.000[e]
	Residual	3.093	31	.100		
	Total	7.360	36			

Figure 10.4 ANOVA in regression

Finally, there is the **Coefficient** table (Figure 10.5) which reports the information pertaining to each individual independent variable. It makes us able to see to what extent each independent variable has predicted the variance in the dependent variable.

In this table, you should first consider the **Sig.** column. Then for each independent variable that has a significant value (less than P-value), consider the column labeled as **Beta**. It indicates the effect that one standard deviation unit change in the independent variable has on the dependent variable. For example, if for a significant independent variable, the reported Beta is .74, it means that one standard deviation unit change in the scores for that independent variable would result in .74 units of change in the dependent variable.

Coefficients[a]

Model		Unstandardized Coefficients		Standardized Coefficients	t	Sig.
		B	Std. Error	Beta		
1	(Constant)	48.261	88.478		.545	.593
	MLAT	12.688	2.844	.712	4.462	.000
	HoursStudy	9.503	7.286	.212	1.304	.211
	Gender	-12.454	33.223	-.060	-.375	.713

a. Dependent Variable: TOEFL

Figure 10.5 Coefficients in regression

Review questions

1. What are the two main types of regression? What are the differences?
2. When we are allowed to use regression?
3. An M.A student is going to investigate the relation between self-regulation and motivation with the writing performance of Persian EFL learners. She understood that there is a significant relationship between the two independent variables (motivation and self-regulation) and the writing performance. Now she wishes to determine which of the independent variables is a better predictor of writing performance. What statistical test can help her? Why? Run the program for the following data and report the findings?

Stude nt	SRL 1	SRL 2	SRL 3	SRL 4	SRL 5	M 1	M 2	M 3	M 4	M 5	Writi ng score
A	1	4	4	3	2	2	1	4	5	3	35

B	1	3	4	2	3	3	3	3	4	5	33
C	4	2	3	2	3	5	2	5	3	2	40
D	4	4	1	3	4	4	2	4	1	3	29
E	3	3	3	1	1	5	5	3	3	5	38
F	3	4	4	1	3	2	4	4	2	1	38
G	2	2	3	4	2	1	4	5	2	5	40

CHAPTER TEN
Non-parametric tests

Preliminaries

The statistics covered so far in this book are all considered to be among the Parametric tests. The reason why they are called parametric is that they mainly concentrate on specific characteristics of population (that's why they are also named as Inferential statistics or even distribution-free test). However, there are some other techniques, referred to as Non-parametric tests which are on the opposite side of parametric tests and are to be dealt with in the present chapter.

Parametric and non-parametric constructs

Parametric statistics try to determine, from the statistics calculated from an actual sample, what the parameters of the population are. In other words, it uses what can actually be measured (the statistics) to estimate what the thing of interest that we can't actually measure it (the parameter). Parametric statistics are based on assuming a certain type of distribution of the data, that is why there are many assumptions about data distribution that need to be met in order to legitimately use parametric statistics. Based on Pett (1997), parametric tests enjoy a set of assumptions the most important of which are as follows:

- Normal distribution of the data
- Specific scales of measurement (interval or continuous data)
- Efficient sample size (usually > 30 per group)
- And equal variance among sample populations

Non-parametric techniques, in contrast, do not require that the data be normally distributed. However, it is not accurate to say that nonparametric tests do not assume homogeneity of variances. But, non-parametric tests like the Kruskal-Wallis assume that population distributions are equal, which would clearly imply that variances are equal as well. Other requirements of non-parametric tests are that sampling is random and observations are independent. However, it doesn't mean that non-parametric tests lack any assumption. Pett (1997) also stated a range of assumptions for these often-belittled tests of which the three most important ones are:

- Less conditions on the population distribution
- Less degrees of stringency on sample size
- Using either nominal (categorical) or ordinal (rank-ordered) scales

Further, Hollander and Wolf (1999) enumerated a bunch of advantages for non-parametric tests:

- Less limitations on the part of population
- Exact estimation of P-value
- The easy-to-application of these tests
- Their easiness to interpret
- Not being sensitive to outlying observations

Knowing the basic assumptions and advantages of non-parametric tests, now the big question is when to use non-parametric tests. Running through the related materials on the same issue, the following pre-requisites can be mentioned which implicate the use if non-parametric tests:

- Nominal and ordinal variables
- Small sample size
- Unequal variance among the groups
- Data containing outliers
- Non-normal distribution of data

In a nutshell, we are recommended to use non-parametric tests when one or more assumptions of parametric tests are violated.

Types of non-parametric tests

Among the numerous types of non-parametric tests, the main four ones are explained in the following. However, prior to that, a brief description is provided as to different non-parametric tests.

Chi-Square Test: Tabulates a variable into categories and computes a chi-square statistic based on the differences between observed and expected frequencies.

Binomial Test: Compares the observed frequency in each category of a dichotomous variable with expected frequencies from the binomial distribution.

Runs Test: Testing whether the order of occurrence of two values of a variable is random.

One-Sample Kolmogorov-Smirnov Test: Compares the observed cumulative distribution function for a variable with a specified theoretical distribution, which may be normal, uniform, exponential, or Poisson.

Two-Independent-Samples Tests: Compares two groups of cases on one variable. The Mann-Whitney U test, two-sample Kolmogorov-Smirnov test, Moses test of extreme reactions, and Wald-Wolfowitz runs test are available.

Two-Related-Samples Tests: Compares the distributions of two variables. The Wilcoxon signed-rank test, the sign test, and the McNemar test are a few examples.

Tests for Several Independent Samples: Compares two or more groups of cases on one variable. The Kruskal-Wallis test, the Median test, and the Jonckheere-Terpstra test are a few examples.

Tests for Several Related Samples: Compare the distributions of two or more variables. Friedman's test, Kendall's W, and Cochran's Q are some examples. Quartiles and the mean, standard deviation, minimum, maximum, and number of nonmissing cases are available for all of the above tests.

Chi-square test: a test of relationships

Chi-square test is perhaps the most often used type of non-parametric test. The Chi-Square Test procedure tabulates a variable into categories and computes a chi-square statistic. This goodness-of-fit test compares the observed and expected frequencies in each category to test that all categories contain the same proportion of values or test that each category contains a user-specified proportion of values. A chi-square test, in other words, investigates whether there is a relationship between two categorical variables. The question is whether there is a relationship between the number of people in each category. For example, we want to see if males and females differ in their choice of foreign language to study in high school, where the school offers Japanese, Spanish, and French. The variable of gender (with two **levels** or two groups inside the variable) is categorical, as is choice of foreign language (with three levels).

A chi-square test for independence has the following attributes:

- It has exactly two variables.
- Each variable has two or more levels (categories) within it, so that the variable name is a word that generalizes (for example gender, experimental group, L1 background).
- You cannot calculate averages of the variables; you can only count how many of them are present in each category.
- All variables are categorical.
- The variables cannot necessarily be defined as independent and dependent (having a cause-and-effect structure), although they might be.

How to obtain Chi-square in SPSS

When you have two or more categorical variables, a simple frequency table will not be adequate to capture the complexity of the situation, especially the interactions of the variables. In this case, a cross-tabulation (crosstabs) is used. In SPSS, crosstabs is the first step toward performing a chi-square. To do so, use the **Analyze** from the menu; then select **Descriptive statistics**; and finally, click on **Crosstabs** menu. You'll see the dialogue box in Figure 9.1. Put one variable each in the **Row(s)** and **Column(s)** boxes. If you have more than two variables, add the additional variables one by one in the

Layer box. In the next step you should click on the **Statistics** choice in the same box and from the newly appeared window select **Chi-square**. After clicking on **Continue** and **OK** buttons, the output tables appears in the output window.

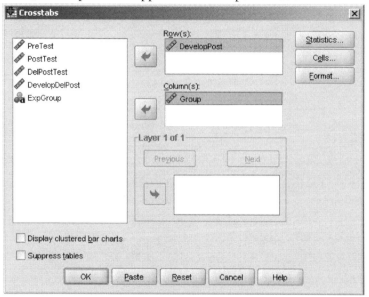

Figure 9.1 Crosstabs window

The final point concerns the results of the chi-square test the interpretations of which are the same as those for other tests (that is, looking at the Sig. value and deciding whether null hypothesis should be rejected).

Mann-Whitney U Test

This kind of non-parametric test is preferable when there are two independent groups and it is intended to see if they are different in terms of an interval variable (and the independent t-test is not appropriate). To obtain this test in SPSS, first select the **Non-parametric test** from the **Analyze** menu. Then click on **2 Independent Sample.** In the box that appears (figure 9-2), move your intended dependent variable into the **Test Variable List** box and your independent variable into the **Grouping Variable**.

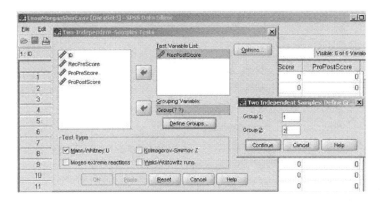

Figure 9.2 Mann-Whitney U Test box

Then like what we did for t-test in defining the groups, define your desired groups. Before clicking on **Continue** and **OK** buttons you should make sure that the **Mann-Whitney U Test** has been ticked in the **Test Type** choice in the same dialogue box.

The main output tables resulted after undergoing the above-steps are two tables like those in figure 9-3 named **Ranks** and **Test statistics** (in different versions of SPSS these tables may be labeled differently). What is of our interest to examine is the amount of Z and P reported as sig. whose interpretation is the same as most other statistics like chi-square.

Mann-Whitney Test

Ranks

	Group	N	Mean Rank	Sum of Ranks
RecPostScore	Non Think Aloud	39	37.01	1443.50
	Think Aloud	38	41.04	1559.50
	Total	77		

Test Statistics[a]

	RecPost Score
Mann-Whitney U	663.500
Wilcoxon W	1443.500
Z	-.799
Asymp. Sig. (2-tailed)	.424

a. Grouping Variable: Group

Figure 9.3 Mann-Whitney U Test results

Wilcoxon signed ranks test

While Mann-Whitney U Test was very similar to independent t-test, Wilcoxon signed ranks test (sometimes referred to as Mc Nemar Test) is very similar to paired t-test. However, in this non-parametric test the scores are converted into ranks and then compared. To gain it in SPSS, after selecting **Non-parametric test** choice from **Analyze** menu, click on **2 Related Samples**. In the opened box (figure 9-4), move the intended paired variables into **Test Pair(s) List**. After that, click on **Wilcoxon** choice in the box labeled **Test Type** and finally **OK**. The results are the same as Mann-Whitney U Test (Z and P value should be checked).

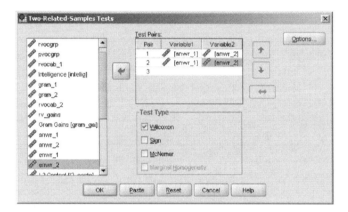

Figure 9.4 Wilcoxon test

Kruskal-Wallis test

It is a non-parametric counterpart to the one-way ANOVA. It should be used when you have one independent variable with three or more levels and one dependent variable. In other words, The Kruskal-Wallis test is an extension of the Mann-Whitney to the case of more than two levels, so the same type of ranking is taking place in this test and the first table of the output will show the rankings of the groups. There is, however, just one problem: just as one-way ANOVA did not provide us with post hoc tests, nor does Kruskal-Wallis. Thus we can't be sure where the putative difference between the groups lies. As a solution to this problem, as Field (2005) suggests, is using separate Mann-Whitney U Test in compensation for lack of post-hoc tests. To calculate this non-parametric test from SPSS, enter the data in the spreadsheet in the same way we entered data for one-way between groups ANOVA. Then, from **Analyze** you should first **Non-parametric tests** and then **K independent sample** (figure 9-5). Then move the desired dependent variable into **Test Variable List** and independent variables into **Grouping variables**. Like the previous cases, make sure you tick the **Kruskal-Wallis H** from **Test Type**. Now you should the range of the independent variables the same as what is done for t-test. However, the difference is that you should here indicate the minimum and maximum values for the groups of your independent variables. To do such an achievement, click on **Define range** and determine the minimum and maximum amounts. The interpretation of the results is the same as what we said.

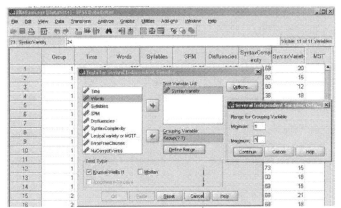

Figure 9.5 Kruskal-Wallis box

Review questions

1. What are the differences between parametric and non-parametric statistical tests?

2. What are the different types of non-parametric tests? Explain briefly.

3. In an experiment where two methods were employed to teach speaking to adults, the numbers of those who improved or did not improve are as follow. What non-parametric test is useful to test the null hypothesis at .05? Why? Run the test and report the results.

4.

	Approach 1	Approach 2
+ improved	46	29
- improved	35	17

CHAPTER ELEVEN

Reliability

Introduction

Having examined the most often-employed statistical analyses, now time is ripe to deal with a topic which is of crucial importance in using any instrument. This significant concept is referred to as "**Reliability**".

Reliability

Reliability analysis allows you to study the properties of measurement scales and the items that compose the scales. The Reliability Analysis procedure calculates a number of commonly used measures of scale reliability and also provides information about the relationships between individual items in the scale. DeVellis (2005) defines reliability as "The proportion of variance in a measure that can be ascribed to a true score" (p. 317). Mackey and Gass (2005) also define reliability as consistency of a score or a test. They say a test is reliable if one and the same person takes it a number of times and get roughly the same score on different administrations of the test. You can see that these two definitions of reliability are similar, for they both address the idea that a test result can be confidently replicated for the same person. Therefore, the more reliable a measurement is, the more precisely it will measure the right thing (the true score) and the less measurement error it will have.

Models of reliability:

There are a set of models and formula which can be used in order to calculate the reliability of something. The most widely used ones are as follows:

- **Alpha (Cronbach):** This model is a model of internal consistency, based on the average inter-item correlation.
- **Split-half:** This model splits the scale into two parts and examines the correlation between the parts.
- **Guttman:** This model computes Guttman's lower bounds for true reliability.
- **Parallel:** This model assumes that all items have equal variances and equal error variances across replications.

- **Strict parallel:** This model makes the assumptions of the Parallel model and also assumes equal means across items.

How to obtain reliability in SPSS

In order to obtain reliability in SPSS you should select **Scale** from **Analyze** menu and then click on **Reliability analysis** choice. In so doing, a dialogue box like the one in figure 8.1 opens.

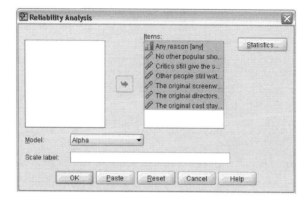

Figure 8.1 Reliability dialogue box

In this box, you should first move your intended items or variables into the box labeled as **Items**. The next step to take is to select your desired model of reliability from the related box in the same box. Finally, click on OK. In the output window, the main table is reliability statistics (figure 8.2) that represents the degree of reliability of your data, instrument, or variable. In this table you should consider the column labeled as **Cronbach's Alpha** (since in this example we chose Cronbach alpha as the reliability index). In the following figure, it is almost 0.88, meaning that there is a high degree of reliability (Cronbach more than .70 is usually considered to be acceptable).

Reliability Statistics

Cronbach's Alpha	Cronbach's Alpha Based on Standardized Items	N of Items
.885	.892	10

Figure 8.2 Reliability statistics output

Reliability analysis statistics

Notice that you can also select various statistics that describe your scale and items. To start such a process, you suffice click on the **Statistics** button in the reliability analysis dialogue box so that a window like figure 8.3 appears.

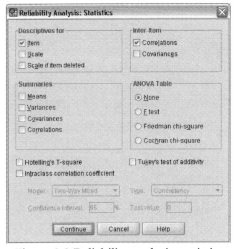

Figure 8.3 Reliability analysis statistics

Statistics included in this box are as follows:

Descriptives for: Produces descriptive statistics for scales or items across cases.

- **Item:** Produces descriptive statistics for items across cases.
- **Scale:** Produces descriptive statistics for scales.
- **Scale if item deleted:** Displays summary statistics comparing each item to the scale that is composed of the other items. Statistics include scale mean and variance if the item were to be deleted from the scale, correlation between the item and the scale that is composed of other items, and Cronbach's alpha if the item were to be deleted from the scale.

Summaries: Provides descriptive statistics of item distributions across all items in the scale.

- **Means:** Summary statistics for item means. The smallest, largest, and average item means, the range and variance of item means, and the ratio of the largest to the smallest item means are displayed.
- **Variances:** Summary statistics for item variances. The smallest, largest, and average item variances, the range and variance of item variances, and the ratio of the largest to the smallest item variances are displayed.
- **Covariances:** Summary statistics for inter-item covariances. The smallest, largest, and average inter-item covariances, the range and variance of inter-item

covariances, and the ratio of the largest to the smallest inter-item covariances are displayed.

- **Correlations:** Summary statistics for inter-item correlations. The smallest, largest, and average inter-item correlations, the range and variance of inter-item correlations, and the ratio of the largest to the smallest inter item correlations are displayed.

Inter-Item: Produces matrices of correlations or covariances between items.

ANOVA Table: Produces tests of equal means.

- **F test:** Displays a repeated measures analysis-of-variance table.
- **Friedman chi-square:** Displays Friedman's chi-square and Kendall's coefficient of concordance. This option is appropriate for data that are in the form of ranks. The chi-square test replaces the usual F test in the ANOVA table.
- **Cochran chi-square:** Displays Cochran's Q. This option is appropriate for data that are dichotomous. The Q statistic replaces the usual F statistic in the ANOVA table.

Review questions

1. What is the importance of reliability? How is it related to factor analysis?
2. Elaborate on the steps to be taken in order to run reliability in SPSS.
3. Consider the following data indicating the scores of a test with 6 items.

	Items					
Student	1	2	3	4	5	6
A	0	1	1	1	1	1
B	1	1	1	0	1	0
C	1	0	0	0	0	0
D	1	0	0	1	1	1
E	0	1	1	1	0	1
F	1	0	1	0	1	1

a) Find the mean, mode, median, and standard deviations for the data.
b) Calculate the reliability for the data and report the results.
c) Find the item discrimination and item facility of the data.

Glossary

95% confidence interval: A range for any parameter that specifies where the true parameter will be found in 95 cases out of 100 if the test were repeated that many times.

Alpha (α): In a regression equation, the alpha is the intercept. It is a constant number that is generated from doing the regression and which is the same for all individuals.

Alpha level (α-level): The point we choose for deciding whether a p-value is extreme or not. In the field of second language research, the alpha level is generally set at $a = .05$.

Alternative hypothesis (H_0): A hypothesis that posits that there is a relationship between variables or that there is a difference between groups. It can be accepted if you can reject the null hypothesis.

Analysis of covariance (ANCOVA): A technique that involves adding a variable to the ANOVA model in order to factor its effects out of the other variables. The covariate added is essentially another independent variable, but it does not enter into any interactions with other variables. Because this is an ANOVA model we are basically interested in seeing whether groups defined by the independent variables performed differently on the dependent variable after the influence of the covariate or covariates has been removed.

Analysis of variance (ANOVA): A model that includes at least one categorical independent variable. We are basically interested in seeing whether groups defined by the independent variable or variables performed differently on the dependent measure.

Bivariate: Using two variables.

Case: Any single collection of values. All the values in a single row. A case is sometimes called a single record, and it normally contains one constant value for each variable.

Case summary: A simple table that directly summarizes values of the cases.

Categorical variable: A type of variable that can take on only one of a specific set of values, such as year of birth, make of car, or favorite color — in effect, defining a category. See also *scale, ordinal, nominal.*

Chart: See *graph.*

Chi-square test: A non-parametric test which uses only nominal data for both the dependent and the independent variable. It tests whether there is a relationship between two variables. This test is not the only one which is based on the chi-square distribution (some of the non-parametric tests in Chapter 14 are as well), but this test has become known as the chi-square test.

Coefficient of determination: A statistic used to specify the correctness of the fit of regression coefficients.

Confidence interval: The range of values around a statistic such as the mean that defines the range where the true population value of the statistic will be found on repeated testing of the research question, with 95% confidence.

Continuous variable: A group of data measured with numbers that have a large range of possible answers. A continuous variable is opposed to a categorical variable.

Correlation: The degree of similarity or difference between two variables.

Data: In order to conduct a statistical analysis you need information, and this is your data. You obtain data by conducting some type of experiment or analysis. Statistical analysis can only be used with quantitative data, or data which can be measured (not all data can!). Data comes in different forms, and may be measured by different types of variables—categorical, ordinal, or interval.

Data Editor: The first window that SPSS brings up when you open the program; it is the area that looks like a spreadsheet, where the data are entered.

Data view: One of the tabs in the Data Editor of SPSS. This is where you see the data arranged with columns representing variables and rows representing individual data observations (usually participants in second language research).

Degrees of freedom: A number that is reported in conjunction with a statistic and specifies the number of components that are free to be chosen. Think of a bowl of ten marbles—how much freedom is there to choose the first marble? There are ten choices. For the second marble, there are only nine choices. By the tenth marble, there are no choices—you must pick the last marble. Therefore, there are $10 - 1 = 9$ degrees of freedom for choosing the order of the marbles in.

Dependent variable: A variable that has its value derived from one or more other variables. Also called a *predicted variable*. See also *independent variable*.

Descriptive statistics: Statistics such as the mean, median, and standard deviation, which are calculated from the sample of people (or texts or test scores) who participated in the experiment.

Dichotomous variable: A variable with only two choices. This will by necessity be an ordinal or categorical variable, not a continuous variable.

Directional test: See *One-tailed test*.

Effect size: An effect size measures how much effect can be attributed to the influence of an independent variable on a dependent variable, or to the relationship between variables. Effect sizes do not depend on sample size. Basically effect sizes tell you how important your statistical result is (whether it is "statistically significant" or not). Measures include Cohen's *d*, partial eta-squared, Pearson's *r*, and R2.

Frequency distribution: The collection of values that a variable takes in a sample.

Graph: A non-numeric display of values. The terms *graph* and *chart* are used in SPSS internal documentation almost interchangeably.

Histogram: A graphical display of a distribution in which the extent of each rectangle represents the magnitude (as in a bar chart) and the width of each rectangle represents the magnitude of the bin. The area of each rectangle thus represents the frequency.

Hypothesis: A formal statement of what you expect to find when you conduct your experiment.

Independent-samples t-test: A parametric test which can tell you whether scores of two separate groups on one measure are statistically different from one another.

Independent variable: A variable whose values are used as the basis for calculation of statistics. See also *dependent variable.*

Inferential statistics: Statistics that generalize to the population that a sample was randomly drawn from, meaning that the results of a statistical test may be generalized to a wider group of people (or texts or test scores) than just those who participated in the experiment.

Likert scale: A scale often used in questionnaires that asks participants to rate some idea using a range of numbers, usually not more than 10. A typical Likert scale may have five points, where 1=strongly agree, 2=somewhat agree, 3=neutral, 4=somewhat disagree, and 5=strongly disagree. Most researchers treat this type of data as interval data, although strictly speaking it may not be.

Linearity An assumption in a correlation is that the relationship between two variables can best be described by a straight line, and this is the assumption of linearity. I have suggested that the best way to assess this assumption is visual comparison of a regression line against a Loess line.

Linear: A straight line. No curves.

Mann–Whitney U test: A non-parametric alternative to the independent-samples ttest. It is used when you have an independent variable with just two groups and one dependent variable. It is essentially the same as the Wilcoxon rank-sum test.

MANOVA: This stands for multivariate analysis of variance. This is used when you want to examine the effects of more than one related dependent variable at a time.

Matched-samples t-test: See *Paired-samples t-test.*

Mean: 1. Another word for average. 2. A calculated value equally distant from the two extreme values. 3. The temperament of the person making you learn this stuff.

Median: The point at which 50% of the scores are higher and 50% of the scores are lower.

Missing data: If you declare a value for a variable as representing the fact that no value is present, the missing value will not be included in calculations.

Mode: The value that occurs most frequently in a given set of data. See also *mean.*

Model: a mathematical model of some process.

Multiple regression: A test used when you have two or more continuous variables and one is the response variable (dependent variable) and one or more are explanatory variables (independent variables). The point of a multiple regression is to find out how much of the variance in scores the explanatory variables explain and/or predict future performance on the response variable.

Multivariate: Using multiple variables.

Nominal: Numbers that specify categories. For example, yes, no, and undecided could be represented by 2, 1, and 0. See also *scale, ordinal,* and *categorical.*

Nonlinear: Not in a straight line. Curved.

Non-parametric statistics: Statistics which do not depend on the data having a normal distribution, but which still impose assumptions on data distribution, such as the requirement that variances be equal across groups. Examples are the Mann–Whitney U test and the Kruskal–Wallis one-way ANOVA.

Normal distribution: A distribution of data where the probability curve follows a bell-curve-shaped distribution. Normal distributions are symmetric around their mean. The requirement for a normal distribution is exact; the data must come from this particular distribution. However, verifying this fact with small sample sizes is usually impossible.

Normality: The degree to which the values match *normal distribution.*

Normal distribution: A distribution that is continuous and symmetric. It is used primarily because many quantitative measurements appear to approximate this distribution. It is also called the bell curve.

One-tailed test: Returns a probability that the sample statistic could be as extreme as or larger than only either the positive or negative value of the statistic. In other words, it uses only one side of the distribution to test the hypothesis. One-tailed tests should be used with caution and mostly if there has been previous research showing the direction of influence, but they can give you more power to find differences.

One-way ANOVA: A parametric test that has one dependent variable (such as score on a test) and one independent variable (such as experimental group). It is usually used when there are three or more levels in the independent variable, but can be used when there are only two (in which case a t-test could also be used). The one-way ANOVA asks whether groups differ in their performance on the dependent variable.

Ordinal: Types of numbers that specify the order of occurrences. The ordinal forms of 1, 2, and 3 are first, second, and third. See also *scale, nominal,* and *categorical.*

Outliers: The extreme values of a variable. Generally, they are the five largest and five smallest values.

Paired-samples t-test: A parametric test which can tell you whether scores of two groups where the same people were tested twice are statistically different from one another.

Parameter: The value of a sampling statistic (such as a mean) or a test statistic (such as an r) in the population, not just in the particular sample taken.

Parametric: A procedure that requires one or more seed values that control its processing.

Pearson's Product Moment Correlation: Commonly called Pearson's correlation. It represents the degree of linear relationship between two variables.

Phi (φ): An effect size that can be calculated for a chi-square (all nominal variables) statistical test where both variables have only two levels (they are dichotomous).

Pivot table: A table with names identifying the rows and columns. Swapping the positions of the rows and columns to make the table appear in a different form, but containing the same data, is known as *pivoting* the table. The tables in SPSS Viewer are pivot tables.

Population: The wider group of people (or texts or test scores) that you would like your experiment to say something about. Most of the time authors do not state what their particular population is, and you must infer it. In the second language research field an intended population may be all ESL learners in a particular country, but this may be overreaching if only a few ESL learners at one particular university are tested!

Post hoc: The erroneous conclusion that some condition arises as the result of a previous condition.

Predicted variable: See *dependent variable*.

P-value: The probability that we would find a statistic as large as the one we found if the null hypothesis were true.

Range: A single number which shows the distance between the minimum and maximum points. For example, if the maximum score on a test was 199 and the minimum was 76, the range would be 123. Ranges can be greatly affected by outliers.

Ratio scale: A scale where all the points on the scale are equally distant from one another and there is a true zero point which signifies a lack of that quality. Weight is a good example of a ratio scale.

Regression: Determining the "best fit" equation for the relationship between two variables. See also *dependent variable* and *independent variable*.

Reliability: DeVellis (2005) defines it as the "proportion of variability in a measure ascribed to the true score" (p. 317). Mackey and Gass (2005) define consistency in a test instrument as being a reliable test; in other words, a person would receive the same score if they took the test again. A study should report the reliability of any test instruments used in the study, but reliability is only a valid construct in the sense of the reliability of a test with a certain sample of test takers. Thus, you should not report the reliability of a test given by someone else in lieu of your own reliability statistics.

Research question: A question that you have that has motivated you to conduct research. The research question does not need to be posed as a formal hypothesis; it can just be a common-sense formulation of the question that you hold.

Sample: The actual people (or texts or test scores) who participate in the experiment. They will hopefully be representative of the population you would like to test

Scale: A type of number that uses a standard by which something is measured, such as inches, pounds, dollars, or hours. Another name for scale is *continuous*. See also *ordinal, nominal,* and *categorical*.

Scatterplot: A graphic which plots two interval-level variables against each other; this is an excellent graph for displaying a large amount of information and for showing relationships among variables.

Skewness: A measure of the unevenness of the distribution of data. Positive skewness indicates more high values than low in the distribution; negative skewness indicates more low values than high.

Spearman's rank order correlation: A non-parametric version of Pearson's correlation test. It tests for the possibility of a relationship between two interval-scale variables.

SPSS: Statistical Package for the Social Sciences. The original name of SPSS.

SPSS Viewer: The window that contains SPSS output, including graphs, tables, and statistical tests.

Standard deviation: A calculated indicator of the extent of deviation for a specific collection of data. The value is derived from the variations where the points are compared to a standard bell-shaped curve. It is the square root of the *variance*.

Statistic: A single number calculated in a specific way. Some examples of types of a statistics are sum, *mean, deviation,* and *average*.

Statistics: A collection of statistical values.

t: The number of degrees of freedom. A continuous distribution with density symmetrical around the null value and a bell-shaped curve.

Two-tailed test: Use this when you want to know the probability that the sample statistic could be as extreme as or larger than both the positive and the negative value of the statistic. In other words, it adds together the probabilities that a statistic that extreme would be found on both the left and the right tail of the distribution.

Two-way ANOVA: A parametric test that has exactly two independent variables and one dependent variable. This is also called a factorial ANOVA.

Univariate: A statistic derived from the values of one variable. Examples are *mean, standard deviation,* and sum.

Variable: In statistical software, a place to store constants. A variable can store a number of constants (one for each case). Each case (or row) in SPSS consists of a collection of constant values assigned to variables.

Variable view: One of the tabs in the Data Editor of SPSS. This is where you see the data arranged with rows representing the variables. Columns here let you define things like how many decimals to display and what numbers for a categorical variable refer to.

Variance: The average of the differences between a set of measured values and a set of expected values on a standard bell-shaped curve. It is the square of the *standard deviation*.

Wilcoxon rank-sum test: A non-parametric test alternative to the independent samples t-test that is used when you have one independent variable with two levels and one dependent variable. It is functionally the same as the Mann–Whitney U test.

Wilcoxon signed-ranks test: A non-parametric test alternative to the paired samples t-test that is used when you have two mean scores that are related, by being either from the same group at different times or from the same group taking two different tests.

z-score: A standardized expression of a variable's values. The z-score expresses how many standard deviations each score is away from the mean. This new distribution has a mean of 0 and a standard deviation of 1.

Made in the USA
San Bernardino, CA
17 February 2020